Capacity Building at the Kurdistan Region Statistics Office Through Data Collection

Sponsored by the Kurdistan Regional Government

Shmuel Abramzon
Nicholas Burger
Bonnie Ghosh-Dastidar
Peter Glick
Krishna B. Kumar
Francisco Perez-Arce
Alexandria C. Smith

This research was undertaken within RAND Labor and Population. RAND Labor and Population has built an international reputation for conducting objective, high-quality, empirical research to support and improve policies and organizations around the world. Its work focuses on labor markets, social welfare policy, demographic behavior, immigration, international development, and issues related to aging and retirement with a common aim of understanding how policy and social and economic forces affect individual decision-making and the well-being of children, adults, and families.

The authors of this report are listed in alphabetical order.

Library of Congress Control Number: 2014937297

ISBN: 978-0-8330-8517-7

The RAND Corporation is a nonprofit institution that helps improve policy and decisionmaking through research and analysis. RAND's publications do not necessarily reflect the opinions of its research clients and sponsors.

Support RAND—make a tax-deductible charitable contribution at www.rand.org/giving/contribute.html

RAND OFFICES

SANTA MONICA, CA • WASHINGTON, DC

PITTSBURGH, PA • NEW ORLEANS, LA • JACKSON, MS • BOSTON, MA

CAMBRIDGE, UK • BRUSSELS, BE

www.rand.org

Preface

Comprehensive and reliable statistics on a region make it possible to identify pressing needs, track progress, plan future development, and create successful policies. The Kurdistan Region of Iraq (KRI) lacks the statistics it needs to improve infrastructure, encourage development, attract investment, and sustain economic growth.

In a previous study, we assessed existing institutional arrangements for collecting and sharing data within the Kurdistan Regional Government (KRG); assessed the data and information infrastructure available in the KRI; identified KRG policy priorities to ensure that collected data are relevant to policymaking; identified data items that need to be collected for each priority area; and recommended data collection methods, institutional arrangements, and a roadmap for implementing recommendations, including steps needed to build human-resource capacity within the KRG and the Kurdistan Regional Statistics Organization (KRSO).[1]

The KRG-funded follow-up study documented here aimed to provide assistance in implementing the recommendations made during the course of the efforts just described. The overarching goal of this study was to assist the KRI's central statistical organization—the KRSO—and the KRG in building the capacity to undertake the recommended data collection. We worked closely with the KRSO and in consultation with relevant ministries to prepare, conduct, and analyze from start to finish a survey critical to KRG policymaking, the Kurdistan Region Labor Force Survey. This survey will make possible ongoing monitoring of trends in labor force participation, unemployment, and other indicators for the region. The RAND Corporation provided the KRSO with overall guidance and analytical and hands-on training. Further, by being involved in the complete life cycle of the survey, from conception through data collection to policy analysis, and by being responsible for the final execution and analysis of the surveys, KRSO staff benefited from learning by doing.

The primary intended audience for this report is KRG policymakers and KRSO staff. The report is intended to serve this audience as (1) a summary of our activities for this project, (2) a presentation of key results from the labor force survey, and (3) a reference guide. By relegating most of the technical details to appendixes, we also aim to make this report accessible to general readers who may be interested in the KRI economy; how capacity building for central statistical organizations can be carried out; and in the design, implementation, and analysis of labor force surveys, especially in the context of emerging economies.

This research was undertaken within RAND Labor and Population. RAND Labor and Population has built an international reputation for conducting objective, high-quality, empiri-

[1] Sandra H. Berry, Nicholas Burger, Harun Dogo, Krishna B. Kumar, Alessandro Malchiodi, Jeffrey Martini, Tewodaj Mengistu, Howard J. Shatz, Alexandria C. Smith, Artur Usanov, and Joanne K. Yoong, *Designing a System for Policy-Relevant Data Collection for the Kurdistan Region-Iraq*, Santa Monica, Calif.: RAND Corporation, MG-1184-KRG, January 2012.

cal research to support and improve policies and organizations around the world. Its work focuses on labor markets, social welfare policy, demographic behavior, immigration, international development, and issues related to aging and retirement with a common aim of understanding how policy and social and economic forces affect individual decisionmaking and the well-being of children, adults, and families. For more information on RAND Labor and Population please contact: RAND Labor and Population, RAND Corporation, 1776 Main Street, P.O. Box 2138, Santa Monica, CA 90407-2138, (310) 393-0411.

More information about RAND is available on our website: http://www.rand.org.

Contents

APPENDIXES[1]

[1] Additional appendixes are available online.

Figures

Tables

Summary

Comprehensive and reliable statistics are crucial for designing economic policies. They make it possible to identify the most pressing needs, track the progress of current policies and initiatives, and plan future development. Most importantly, statistics are a major part of the foundation for successful policy planning in many areas. The Kurdistan Region of Iraq (KRI) lacks the statistics it needs to improve infrastructure, encourage private sector development, attract foreign investment, and create sustained economic growth.

In a previous study, we

- assessed the Kurdistan Regional Government's (KRG's) existing institutional arrangements for collecting and sharing data
- assessed the data and information infrastructure currently available in the KRI
- identified the KRG's policy priorities to ensure the collection of relevant data for policymaking
- identified data items that need to be collected for each priority area, highlighting those that are most critical for policymakers at the highest level
- recommended data collection methods and institutional arrangements and provided a roadmap for implementing the recommendations, including the steps needed to build human-resource capacity within the KRG and the Kurdistan Regional Statistics Organization (KRSO).[1]

The work documented in this volume aimed to assist implementation of the recommendations from the previous study. The overarching purpose was to help the KRI central statistical organization—the KRSO—and the KRG build the capacity to undertake the recommended data collection. RAND worked closely with the KRSO and in consultation with relevant ministries to prepare, conduct, and analyze, from start to finish, the first round of a survey critical to KRG policymaking, the Kurdistan Region Labor Force Survey (KRLFS). The survey will be conducted quarterly to enable ongoing monitoring of labor force participation, unemployment, and other important indicators for the region. RAND provided the KRSO with overall guidance and both analytical and hands-on training. Further, by being involved in the complete life cycle of the survey, from conception through data collection to policy analysis, and by being responsible for the final execution and analysis of the surveys, KRSO staff benefited from learning by doing.

[1] Sandra H. Berry, Nicholas Burger, Harun Dogo, Krishna B. Kumar, Alessandro Malchiodi, Jeffrey Martini, Tewodaj Mengistu, Howard J. Shatz, Alexandria C. Smith, Artur Usanov, and Joanne K. Yoong, *Designing a System for Policy-Relevant Data Collection for the Kurdistan Region–Iraq*, Santa Monica, Calif.: RAND Corporation, MG-1184-KRG, 2012

The project involved the following activities, with capacity building being deeply involved in all:

1. design of the KRLFS sampling approach
2. development of the survey questionnaire
3. data collection, cleaning, and validation
4. analysis of KRLFS data to assess key labor force indicators
5. development of recommendations for a KRI establishment survey that would enable the calculation of a reliable measure of gross domestic product for the KRI.

Activities 1 through 4 were carried out in close collaboration with the KRSO during a series of five intensive workshops held at KRSO headquarters (with attendance ranging from 15 to 30 staff) and through frequent communications over the life of the project.

The KRSO carried out the first KRLFS round successfully in July 2012 and the second in December 2012. Existing capacity was enhanced through workshops and learning by doing. Analysis of the data from the first round highlighted a number of important characteristics of the KRI labor force and economy, including low overall participation in the labor force, especially of women; an overall unemployment rate (7.4 percent) that is low relative to those of most countries in the Middle East; significantly higher unemployment among youth and among women; the dominance of the public sector as a source of employment and the contrasting small role of the formal private sector; and the predominant role of service-sector employment, which accounts for three-quarters of all work, compared with less than 20 percent for industry.

Future rounds of the KRLFS will provide up-to-date information on how these and other important indicators are changing over time and in response to policies. At the same time, continued implementation of the survey is likely to help to enhance the KRSO's capabilities in data collection, analysis, and reporting and build skills and experience for other survey collection efforts to meet specific needs for information.[2]

---

[2] Since the KRSO will take primary responsibility for the analysis of the second and future rounds of the survey, they are not discussed here.

Acknowledgments

We are grateful to the Kurdistan Regional Government (KRG) for supporting this research. Although we benefited immensely from the feedback and support we received from numerous KRG officials, we are particularly indebted to His Excellency Ali Sindi, Minister of Planning; Serwan Mohamed, Director of the Kurdistan Regional Statistics Office; and Zagros Fatah, General Director, Ministry of Planning.

We could not have met as many KRG officials as we did during our visits to the KRI without the unceasing efforts of and translation services provided by Wirya Mahmood, Omar Abit, Hoshyar Tahsin, and Farhad Borhan Qadir. We are also grateful for the advice and input we received from the teams of other studies RAND conducted for the KRG. These were led by C. Ross Anthony, Melinda Moore, Howard J. Shatz, Louay Constant, Georges Vernez, Shelly Culbertson, and Robin Meili.

We also want to acknowledge the talented and dedicated staff of the KRSO, whose hard work made the first Kurdistan Regional Labor Force Survey a success. In particular, we would like to thank Gohdar Mohammad Ali Saeid, Raqeeb Bahaadin Mohammed, Saman Ahmad, Fatma Omer Ali, Bashdar Ayub Kareem, Soran Habib, Shwan Abbas Khudhur, and Nahema Akram Jabar.

At RAND, we benefited from the guidance and support of the Labor and Population Unit. We are also grateful to Robin Meili, Director of International Programs, who coordinated the suite of RAND studies, and to Parisa Roshan and Joy Moini, who assisted her. We also thank Sarah Weilant for her work on formatting the draft of this report, and RAND's editorial staff for their help with the final product.

Finally, the report has benefited from the insightful comments of two anonymous reviewers.

Abbreviations

2012Q3	third quarter of 2012
CSO	Central Statistical Organization
DEFF	design effect
ESS	effective sample size
GDP	gross domestic product
GRP	gross regional product
ICC	intracluster correlation coefficient
IHSES	Iraq Household Socio-Economic Survey
IKN	Iraq Knowledge Network
ILO	International Labour Organization
ISCO	International Standard Classification of Occupations
KRG	Kurdistan Regional Government
KRI	Kurdish Region of Iraq
KRLFS	Kurdistan Region Labor Force Survey
KRSO	Kurdistan Regional Statistics Organization
LFP	labor force participation
ME	margin of error
PSU	primary sampling unit
RG	rotation group
SRS	simple random sampling
SSU	secondary sampling unit

Glossary

cluster design	A sampling approach that begins with random selection of primary sampling units (PSUs) in the KRI blocks from the census frame. Once the PSUs are selected, a sample of households is randomly selected within each PSU. The households are known as the secondary sampling units (SSUs).
confidence interval	Calculated for a statistic (such as the unemployment rate) that shows the range around that statistic within which the true value will lie with a specified level of probability, typically 95 percent.
design effect (DEFF)	The conversion factor going from a sample size needed under simple random sampling (SRS) to a complex design, such as a cluster design. DEFF is the ratio of the variance of an estimate obtained via the complex design over the variance of the same estimate obtained under an SRS. When the DEFF is greater than 1, it is less precise than the SRS. The DEFF for national-level estimates includes a second adjustment over and above the one done for clustered design. This effect arises from using unequal sample weights for different strata.
disproportionate sample allocation	A sample allocation strategy that samples at a higher rate in smaller districts, causing them to be overrepresented in the sample (and causing larger districts to be somewhat underrepresented). Contrast with proportionate-to-size sample allocation.
effective sample size (ESS)	The sample size required under SRS.
equal sample allocation	A type of disproportionate sample allocation strategy, in which the same number of households or individuals is drawn from each stratum, e.g., from each district.
explicit stratification	A sampling scheme that divides the population into strata—for example, by district or by rural and urban location of residence. Separate samples are then randomly selected from each stratum. This ensures that each stratum is adequately represented in the sample. Contrast with SRS.

intracluster correlation coefficient (ICC)	Measures the correlations of outcomes among units within a cluster. If individuals are organized into "groups," (i.e., survey clusters) and we divide the total variance in the outcome into variation that is "within groups" and "between groups," then the ICC is the proportion of the total variance that is "between groups."
margin of error (ME)	One-half the width of the confidence interval.
nominal sample size	The total or actual sample size required to obtain a given level of precision, which is obtained by multiplying the effective sample size with the DEFF.
proportionate-to-size sample allocation	A scheme that allocates to each district the same share of the sample as its share of the overall population by applying a common sampling rate (or percentage of households) to all districts. Contrast with disproportionate sample allocation.
simple random sampling (SRS)	A sampling scheme that draws the random sample from the population as a whole. Contrast with explicit stratification.
stratum	A subgroup of homogeneous (similar) units within the larger population for which the key statistics are to be calculated.

CHAPTER ONE

Introduction

Comprehensive and reliable statistics are crucial for policy formulation in any region or country. Statistics make it possible to identify the most pressing needs, track progress of current policies and initiatives, and plan future development. Most importantly, statistics are the foundation for successful policy planning in many areas. The Kurdistan Region of Iraq (KRI) lacks the statistics it needs to improve infrastructure, encourage private-sector development, attract foreign investment, and create sustained economic growth. For instance, high youth unemployment rates in the Middle East have led to mounting frustration and social unrest. Unemployment was a key concern of the Kurdistan Regional Government (KRG), but the government did not have reliable unemployment data for the KRI, let alone the youth unemployment rate, which allow it to diagnose any existing problems and develop policies to address them.

This report summarizes the results of a study that built on previous RAND Corporation efforts to design a policy-relevant data collection system for the KRI.[1] In the current project, we provided assistance in implementing the recommendations made in the previous work. The project's overarching objective has been to help the central statistical organization of the KRI—the Kurdistan Regional Statistics Organization (KRSO)—and the KRG build the capacity to undertake policy-relevant data collection. RAND worked closely with the KRSO to prepare, conduct, and analyze—from start to finish—labor force surveys critical to KRG policymaking. RAND provided overall guidance and both analytical and hands-on training. Because KRSO staff members were involved in the complete life cycle of the survey, from conception through data collection to policy analysis, and because they were responsible for the final execution and analysis of the surveys, they learned by doing.

Data Collection in the Kurdistan Region of Iraq

In our previous project to support data collection for policymaking in the KRI, RAND conducted the following tasks:

- assessed the KRG's current institutional arrangements for collecting and sharing data
- assessed the data and information infrastructure currently available in the KRI

---

[1] Sandra H. Berry, Nicholas Burger, Harun Dogo, Krishna B. Kumar, Alessandro Malchiodi, Jeffrey Martini, Tewodaj Mengistu, Howard J. Shatz, Alexandria C. Smith, Artur Usanov, and Joanne K. Yoong, *Designing a System for Policy-Relevant Data Collection for the Kurdistan Region–Iraq*, Santa Monica, Calif.: RAND Corporation, MG-1184-KRG, January 2012.

- identified the KRG's policy priorities to ensure the collection of relevant data for policymaking
- identified data items that need to be collected for each priority area, highlighting those that are critical for policymakers at the highest level
- recommended data collection methods and institutional arrangements and provided a roadmap for implementing recommendations, including the steps needed to build human resource capacity within the KRG and the KRSO.

The KRG and KRSO have already made great strides in developing a robust data-collection system. They are in a good position to build on the progress made to date, to implement new data-collection activities, and to increase institutional capacity. Priorities we identified for the KRI include developing a system of high-quality labor force and enterprise surveys. Making these and other data available to policymakers in a transparent and timely manner will help the KRG achieve its policy goals.

Through discussions with the KRG Minister of Planning, the KRSO director, and various ministries, RAND and the KRSO identified two general needs for this project to address:

1. the need for data collection through surveys and other means and analysis of the collected data
2. the need for KRSO staff to be involved in the complete survey process (sampling, questionnaire design, implementation of the survey, and data analysis) and to develop the capacity for the KRSO to independently carry out each of these aspects of survey work.

We believe that working with the KRSO to execute the survey process from start to finish addressed these needs and will produce both increased capacity within the KRSO and tangible data outputs that should enhance the KRG's ability to make informed policy decisions.

The remainder of this chapter describes the outline of the project RAND conducted in partnership with the KRSO to meet these objectives.

Improving Data Collection Through Capacity Building

Capacity building through working collaboratively with the client is a role RAND has played for many public- and private-sector organizations around the world and is increasingly playing for ministries and quasigovernmental entities in the Middle East.

The effort took place over approximately 12 months and included two rounds of an unemployment survey (the first in July 2012, the second in December 2012) and development of recommendations for an establishment survey that can supply data for calculating the KRI's gross regional product (GRP). The core project tasks, which subsequent chapters describe in detail, included

- design the sampling approach for the Kurdistan Region Labor Force Survey (KRLFS)
- develop the labor force survey questionnaire, working closely with the KRSO
- collect the KRLFS data, then clean and validate the data
- analyze the KRLFS data to assess key labor force outcomes
- make recommendations for a KRI establishment survey.

The project produced multiple deliverables, which we reference throughout the report. In addition to this final report for the KRG, we produced templates for reporting data to the public (and possibly for the KRG's internal use), as is the common practice among established statistical agencies.

Workshops to Support Capacity Building

RAND team members with expertise in survey data collection and analysis methods, conducted a total of five workshops for the KRSO staff and other government analysts over three separate trips to the KRI. The KRSO staff can refer to the workshop presentations, which are offered in online appendixes to this document, during future rounds of the KRLFS and other surveys. The workshops were designed to be instructive and interactive. Figure 1.1 shows the five steps of the survey process, each of which was the subject of a separate workshop.

The workshops were closely integrated with the development and implementation of the KRLFS and were designed and timed to coincide with critical steps in the survey process. For example, the sampling and questionnaire workshops took place early in the project, when RAND and the KRSO were preparing to work jointly to design the questionnaire and set up the sampling structure.

The Kurdistan Region Labor Force Survey

The primary activity of the project was to work closely with the KRSO to develop, implement, and analyze the first round of a recurring, periodic labor force survey in the KRI. The survey was designed and executed in a way that met multiple KRG goals:

- The questionnaire was developed according to international best practices, including International Labour Organization (ILO) guidelines for measuring labor force characteristics. This ensures both that the data are of high quality and that they can be used for international comparisons.
- The sampling approach was developed to provide both breadth and depth: The sample size is large enough to produce estimates for KRI-level statistics with exceptionally high precision and allow subgroup and district-level analysis with moderate precision or better.
- The survey was designed and set up to be implemented on a recurring, quarterly basis. This will ultimately provide the government and public in the KRI with reliable, regularly updated information on the labor force and labor market conditions to support policy decisionmaking.

Subsequent chapters describe the components of the labor force survey in greater detail.

Figure 1.1
The Survey Process and the Structure of RAND Workshops for the KRSO

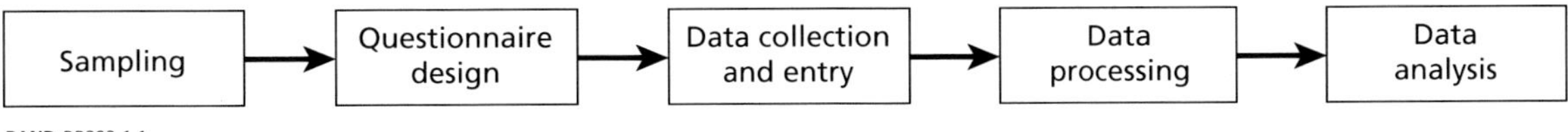

RAND *RR293-1.1*

Survey Time Line and Frequency

Since the first round of the KRLFS was designed from scratch, we spent a full six months with the KRSO designing the sampling scheme and the questionnaire. Capacity-building workshops took place during this time. The KRSO collected and cleaned the data over two months and then analyzed the cleaned data during the subsequent two months. For future rounds, as the staff gain more experience, the time needed for the sampling and questionnaire design phases should be shorter, as should that for the analysis phase. The process will also speed up as experience leads to adjustments to the sampling frame, questionnaires, field logistics, and analysis approaches.

While quarterly surveys provide up-to-date information and capture the dynamics of the labor market effectively, they are resource intensive and are best instituted after the requisite capacity is built. The KRLFS was set up with the goal of becoming a quarterly survey. However, in its first two years, resource and capacity constraints have made it necessary to conduct the survey every six months. As the survey team continues to gain experience and as the KRSO planning process adapts to scheduling the survey more frequently, the quarterly schedule should be attainable.

Recommendations for an Establishment Survey

The second component of the project was to scope out and provide a framework for a future KRI-wide survey of establishments. Data from a survey of establishments would be a useful input into the calculation of GRP, or total output, of the KRI. The actual implementation of this survey and the use of the data to calculate GRP were beyond the scope of this project, especially given the primary focus on developing the labor force surveys. Nevertheless, the survey development work done here will feed directly into future GRP calculation activities. Our work here focused on using cross-country comparisons to identify best practices in firm survey data collection that can be used to calculate gross domestic product (GDP) in the KRI. A number of countries, including the United States, use establishment surveys to also collect labor market information, such as employment, hours, and earnings of employees, which can be used to get a range of employment estimates, although such surveys are not useful for the calculation of labor force participation or unemployment rates. Based on our analysis, we made recommendations for modifying the establishment survey currently under consideration by the KRSO and the Central Statistical Organization (CSO).

Organization of This Report

Most of the remainder of this report provides greater detail on the critical steps that RAND and the KRSO followed in carrying out this large-scale representative survey. Chapter Two summarizes the development of a robust and effective sampling strategy for the KRLFS. Chapter Three reviews the questionnaire design process, which drew on international best practices while, at the same time, customizing the survey to the particular needs and labor market conditions of the KRI. Chapter Four provides a brief summary of the data collection process for the first round of the KRLFS, which the KRSO led. Chapter Five summarizes the process of analyzing the data and presents key labor force statistics generated from the first KRLFS. Chapter Six turns to the establishment survey work and provides recommendations based on international comparisons to inform the design of a future establishment survey that could be used to construct regional GDP estimates for the KRI. Chapter Seven concludes with a summary of the report and a look ahead.

In addition to the two appendixes in this volume, which discuss KRLFS sampling procedures, a separate document is available online that contains multiple appendixes presenting the KRLFS survey instrument and detailed information on the workshops RAND conducted throughout the project.

CHAPTER TWO

Sampling Design

Objective

Sampling is a critical, and perhaps the most technical, part of designing and conducting a survey. During our discussions with KRSO director Serwan Mohamed at the start of the project, it became clear that building capacity in this area among KRSO staff was important. By working with the staff on the sampling for an actual survey—the KRLFS—and through a two-day sampling design workshop, we sought to build this capacity.

The KRLFS Sampling Design

The KRLFS gathers information on employment and other labor force data from a random sample of households throughout the KRI. Sampling is significantly more cost efficient than gathering information from every individual in the population, as a census would do. The aim of the sampling strategy is to carefully select the sample so that the statistics calculated and reported are truly representative of the KRI population and of relevant regions or subgroups and so that these statistics are "reliable" or "precise," that is, estimated with a high level of certainty. The science of sampling is well developed, and we adopted state-of-the-art techniques to carry out the KRLFS.

The following paragraphs summarize our sampling strategy for the labor force survey. Appendix A provides an in-depth analysis of this strategy and the justifications for using it.

The sampling design was chosen to ensure that statistics, such as the unemployment rate, could be calculated with acceptable precision at the all-KRI level and for the following subgroups: governorate, age groups (15–30, 31–49, 50–64), gender, urban or rural, gender by urban or rural, age groups by urban or rural, and governorate by urban or rural.

As in previous household surveys in the KRI and Iraq, we followed a two-stage design, with blocks or enumeration areas listed in the census frame serving as the primary sampling units (or survey clusters) and households within them as the secondary sampling units.

We explicitly stratified the sample by each of the 33 districts in the KRI. There are different approaches to determining how many households (units) to sample in each district. *Proportional allocation* sampling allocates the sample across districts in proportion to their share in the overall population. This is desirable from the point of view of precision at the subgroup and national levels but ends up including very few units from the smallest districts and very many from the largest. In contrast, *equal allocation*, a form of *dis*proportionate sampling, chooses the same number of households from all districts, regardless of their size. This approach, which the

Iraq Household Socio-Economic Survey (IHSES) and other surveys use, ensures adequate representation from the smallest districts and equal precision across districts. But when districts are of very different sizes, as with the KRI, the approach seriously decreases precision at the national level because of the need for sampling weights and reduces precision even more at the subgroup level for the larger subgroups.

We therefore adopted, with slight modifications, a compromise approach that Leslie Kish has suggested, which allocates the sample of households *dis*proportionately across districts, ensures a minimum sample size for the smallest districts, and limits the maximum sample size allocated to the largest.[1] Within each district, we selected clusters or blocks randomly, with selection probability proportional to size. That is, the probability of a cluster being selected is proportional to its share of the overall population of the district.

A key part of sampling design is choosing the size of the sample: the larger the number of units or households, the more precise the estimates of unemployment or other statistics, and the more likely it will be possible to generate reliable estimates for different subsamples. At the same time, a larger sample raises the cost and time it takes to carry out the survey. Sample size calculations are used to choose the appropriate sample size and rely on estimates of means and variances of key indicators and of the intracluster correlation coefficient (ICC), which is the correlation of the outcomes of units within a sampling cluster or block. The ICC measures how similar households or individuals are within a block; the higher the ICC, the less efficient the estimates, meaning it takes a larger sample to achieve a given level of precision.

To guide the sample-size calculations, we used data from available sources, especially the most recent available IHSES (2007). The data we used are estimated labor force participation rate in the KRI (mean 42.39 percent, variance 0.49), estimated unemployment rate among those in the labor force (mean 11.9 percent, variance 0.32), and ICCs of 0.0268 and 0.0335 for labor force participation and unemployment, respectively. We also made use of estimates of the average number of individuals per household aged 15 or older in Kurdistan (3.77 in the IHSES) and the average number of labor force participants per household (1.60).

Finally, we calculated the sample sizes that would be needed to obtain different margins of error (MEs)—3 percent, 5 percent, 7.5 percent, and 10 percent—and considered the implications for sample size of having different cluster sizes (households sampled per block). The ME is a measure of how precise or reliable an estimate from a sample is. For example, if the estimated unemployment rate is 6 percent with a 2-percent ME, we can say with 95-percent certainty that the actual unemployment rate falls between 4 percent and 8 percent, i.e., within a range of 2 percentage points below and above the estimate. The larger the sample, all things equal, the smaller the ME, the more reliable the estimates.

We first used the estimates of the labor force and unemployment rates, the ICCs, and the desired maximum ME to calculate the sample size that would be needed if the sampling strategy were simple random sampling. In practice, the two-stage design means we were sampling within clusters or blocks, and because of the ICC, this reduces efficiency or precision (i.e., increases the ME). We converted the initial sample-size estimate under simple random sampling to the actual sample size required using the design effect to account for the clustered design, as well as an additional design effect due to the weighting arising from the nonproportionate allocation across districts described above. Finally, we used the number of individuals

---

[1] Leslie Kish, "Multipurpose Sample Designs," *Survey Methodology*, Vol. 14, No. 1, 1988, pp. 19–32.

per household to convert this desired sample size, which refers to individuals, to the number of required households for the sample.

Our final intended sample size was 7,000 households. The ME for the overall national estimate of labor force participation was predicted by our calculations to be small, about 1.1 percent. The expected ME associated with the overall national estimate of unemployment rate was also about 1.1 percent. Under the modified Kish rule we adopted, the ME at the district level was expected to vary between 3.5 and 5.6 percent for labor force participation and between 3.1 and 5.0 percent for the unemployment rate. The sample size chosen also ensured adequate precision for the various subgroups noted above (governorate, gender, age category). Overall, the proposed sampling scheme was expected to yield high levels of precision for these subgroups: The 5-percent ME was rarely exceeded for the participation and unemployment outcomes, and a stricter 3-percent ME was exceeded only in a few cases. The actual survey data confirmed the overall accuracy of these predictions.

Table 2.1 presents the numbers of sampled households in each of the 33 districts in the KRI. Ten households were interviewed per cluster, so the total number of clusters in each district is the indicated number of households divided by ten.

Finally, since the sample was not a simple random sample, we calculated sampling weights to account for the disproportionate allocation of the sample across districts (weights were also used to adjust for nonresponse). Applying the weights in the analysis restores the representativeness of the sample.

Rotation Group Scheme

In consultation with KRI policymakers, it was decided that a labor survey repeated at regular and frequent intervals would best serve the needs of policymaking by providing up-to-date information on trends in unemployment and other key measures. Following the practice in a number of countries, and discussions with KRI policymakers, a system of quarterly surveys was determined to be a good choice for the KRI. Repeated surveys can entail drawing a new sample of households or individuals in each round or, alternatively, interviewing the same sample over repeated rounds of the survey (a panel survey). Surveying the same households or individuals has several benefits. It significantly increases the precision of estimates of changes in aggregate measures. Further, following the same individuals for multiple periods allows better understanding of changes over time in individual labor force outcomes (participation, hours of work, and earnings).

However, panel surveys also suffer from attrition due to survey fatigue: Over time, more and more households tend to drop out of the sample. When this happens, the sample gets smaller, and, most likely, also less representative; replacing lost households can restore sample size but not representivity.

Rotation designs offer a compromise by allowing some overlap of the sample over survey rounds to increase efficiency, while avoiding a complete overlap that leads to high attrition through excessive reinterviewing. The following outlines the rotation design we recommended to the KRSO for the subsequent waves of the survey:

Table 2.1
Number of Households in the Sample by District, with Districts Ordered by Population

Rank	Governorate	District	Population	Number of Households
1	Erbil	Hawler center	852,329	400
2	Sulaymaniya	Sulaymaniya center	761,557	400
3	Duhok	Duhok center	323,400	350
4	Duhok	Zakho	237,236	280
5	Erbil	Deshti Hawler	203,072	250
6	Sulaymaniya	Raniya	198,518	250
7	Erbil	Makhmur	178,319	240
8	Sulaymaniya	Kalar	170,624	230
9	Duhok	Semel	162,058	230
10	Erbil	Soran	159,969	220
11	Duhok	Akre	152,124	220
12	Sulaymaniya	Chamchamal	145,358	210
13	Duhok	Shekhan	145,043	210
14	Erbil	Shaqlawa	131,660	210
15	Duhok	Bardash	118,841	200
16	Sulaymaniya	Pishdar	114,731	200
17	Duhok	Amedi	95,797	190
18	Erbil	Koye	95,746	190
19	Erbil	Khabat	95,148	190
20	Sulaymaniya	Halabja	91,611	180
21	Sulaymaniya	Sayid Sadiq	73,010	180
22	Sulaymaniya	Dukan	62,881	170
23	Sulaymaniya	Sharezur	58,536	170
24	Erbil	Mergasur	52,865	170
25	Sulaymaniya	Kifri	47,250	170
26	Sulaymaniya	Derbendikhan	43,297	170
27	Sulaymaniya	Penjwin	40,475	160
28	Erbil	Choman	28,404	160
29	Erbil	Rawenduz	22,608	160
30	Sulaymaniya	Sharbjer	18,628	160
31	Sulaymaniya	Khanaqin	11,967	160
32	Sulaymaniya	Qaradakh	7,983	160
33	Sulaymaniya	Mawat	7,839	160
Total			4,909,884	7,000

- The KRLFS will follow a "2-(2)-2" rotation scheme. In this common design, each household is sampled for two consecutive quarters, "rests" for the next two quarters, is sampled again for two quarters, then finally exits the sample.[2]
- In a given round, there are four cohorts or panels, each making up one-quarter (1,750) of the total sample of 7,000 households. Each cohort is interviewed for two consecutive quarters, is out for two more, then is back in for two more. Figure 2.1 shows the flow over time of the cohorts that make up the sample.
- To manage the logistics of this sampling approach, it is useful to divide the sample clusters (700 blocks of ten households each) into two rotation groups (RGs), labeled RG 1 and RG 2. Each RG contains one-half (350) of the sample clusters and one-half (3,500) of the sample households. Two of the four cohorts sampled in a given quarter belong to RG 1, and two belong to RG 2. Figure 2.2 illustrates this process for one district, Soran in Erbil Governorate; as Table 2.1 shows, the sampling scheme allocated this district 22 clusters (hence 220 households). We randomly assign one-half (11) of the clusters in this district to RG 1 and one-half to RG 2. Thus, for the whole sample, we ended up with two RGs with 350 blocks or clusters each, with each district having its clusters divided evenly between RG 1 and RG 2.
- Households in a new cohort are added from the same clusters from which an exiting cohort is being dropped. Given ten households per cluster, there are five households in the old and five in the new cohort; those in the new cohort are chosen from the listing of households *excluding* those from the older cohort.
- Figure 2.1 shows that the sample is built up incrementally with the addition of new cohorts: It takes until year 2, quarter 2 to obtain the full sample of 7,000 households

Figure 2.1
The 2-(2)-2 Rotation Scheme for the KRLFS

Survey Round							1	2	3	4	5	6	7
		Year 1				Year 2				Year 3			
Rotation Group	Cohort/ Panel	1	2	3	4	1	2	3	4	1	2	3	4
1	1 (n=1,750)												
2	2 (n=1,750)												
1	3 (n=1,750)												
2	4 (n=1,750)												
1	5 (n=1,750)												
2	6 (n=1,750)												
1	7 (n=1,750)												
2	8 (n=1,750)												
1	9 (n=1,750)												
2	10 (n=1,750)												
1	11 (n=1,750)												

...

NOTE: Colors represent individual cohorts.
RAND *RR293-2.1*

---

[2] See Eurostat, *Task Force on the Quality of the Labour Force Survey: Final Report*, Luxemburg: Publications Office of the European Union, 2009.

Figure 2.2
Schematic Depiction of Rotation Groups and Cohorts Sample in Survey Round 1 for Soran District, Erbil Governorate

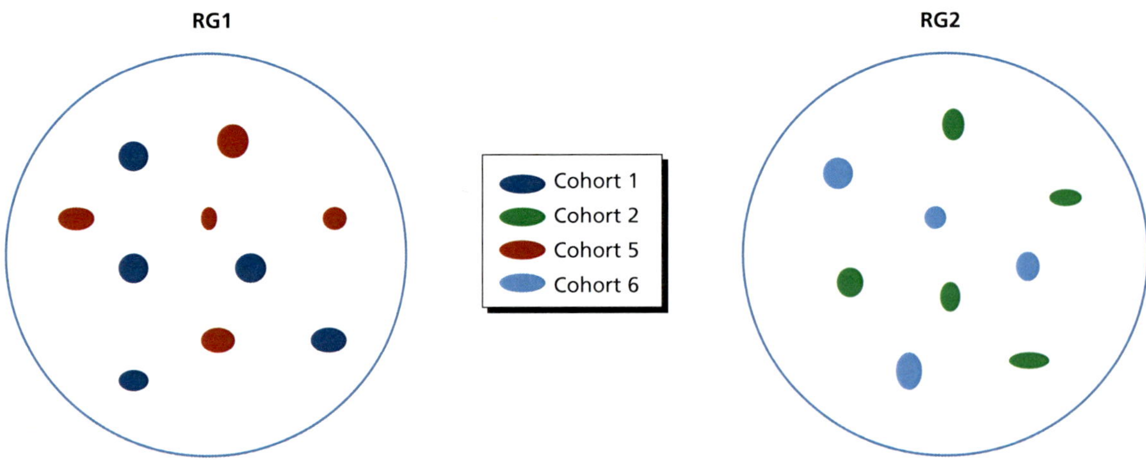

NOTES: Each RG has 11 clusters of ten households, five in each cohort, for 110 households. The orientation, sizes, and shapes of the ovals have no particular significance other than capturing the heterogeneous nature of the different clusters.
RAND *RR293-2.2*

in four cohorts. While this incremental approach is common, it is also possible to begin with the full sample by starting off *as if* the survey were already in this quarter (shown as Survey Round 1 in Figure 2.1). This is advantageous because it provides estimates for the full sample size in the first round. This approach is carried out as follows:

– Create the two RGs as discussed above.
– From each cluster in RG 1, randomly select five households for "cohort 1." Then from the list of remaining households in these clusters, randomly select five households to be in "cohort 5."
– From each cluster in RG 2, randomly select five households for "cohort 2." Then from the list of remaining households in these clusters, randomly select five households to be in "cohort 6."
– All of the households in these four cohorts (a total sample of 7,000) are interviewed in the first round of the survey.

Figure 2.2 depicts this scheme for Soran District in Erbil Governorate. Similar procedures take place in all districts. In the next quarter we act as if we are in year 2, quarter 3, in Figure 2.1, and each cohort is treated accordingly:

- Cohort 1 is treated as if it has already been interviewed four times by the previous quarter, so leaves the survey.
- Cohort 2 is treated as if this quarter is its fourth interview, so continues for this round, then leaves permanently.
- Cohort 5 is treated as if the previous quarter were its second interview, so it leaves this quarter to return two quarters later for two more survey rounds.
- Cohort 6 is treated as if this is its second interview, so after this quarter, it takes a two-quarter break before returning for two more survey rounds.

- Cohort 3 is started in RG 1 clusters (five new households per cluster). This cohort is treated as if it is coming back after being interviewed twice and then will be out for two quarters, so it will be interviewed again next quarter, then leave permanently.
- Cohort 7 is also started in RG 1 clusters (five new households per cluster), for the first of its four survey rounds.

The process continues in future survey rounds, as depicted in Figure 2.1.

Workshops and Capacity Building

Early discussions with the KRSO identified sampling design as a key area for capacity building. Therefore, KRSO staff were involved in the various steps of the sampling design. First, RAND staff conducted an intensive two-day workshop on sampling at the KRSO in February 2012.[3] The topics covered included sampling (probability sampling and stratified and clustered designs), construction and use of sampling weights, sample size considerations, precision (ME), and power.

Following the workshop, in consultation with the KRSO, RAND staff generated the Kish allocation scheme for the districts. The KRSO randomly selected the clusters in each district and households within clusters. The KRSO also selected RGs and cohorts with RAND's guidance. As with each step of the overall survey process, frequent interaction of RAND and KRSO staff ensured that sampling expertise was being transferred to KRSO staff. For instance, KRSO staff, with RAND guidance, generated sampling weights on their own, which RAND then verified. Likewise, for the second round of the survey, the KRSO staff generated RGs and cohorts on their own.

Summary

We helped KRSO staff develop their capacity in sampling design through a workshop, then assisted their design of samples for an actual survey, the KRLFs. The process also resulted in a sampling design that embodies best international practice for labor force surveys and that, through quarterly survey rounds, will provide timely and reliable data to policymakers and the public. Further, since the survey will be repeated every quarter, skills in sampling techniques will be reinforced over time.

---

[3] See Appendix E in the online companion volume for the workshop presentation.

CHAPTER THREE

Questionnaire Design

Activities and Capacity Building for Questionnaire Design

During early meetings with KRSO staff and other key stakeholders, we took stock of challenges and specificities relevant for understanding the KRI labor market and clarified the objectives of the new labor force survey. Taking these factors into consideration, RAND and the KRSO designed the survey instruments for the KRLFS following a workshop on questionnaire design held in Erbil in February 2012. In preparation for designing the questionnaire, RAND and the KRSO reviewed surveys previously conducted in Kurdistan and internationally, considering their strengths and weaknesses and the information gaps that needed to be filled.

As described earlier, the design, implementation, and analysis of the employment survey were closely linked to capacity building at the KRSO. The objective was to work closely with KRSO staff on the survey, so that they learned by doing. The KRSO has extensive experience in organizing fieldwork and carrying out surveys and data entry. Therefore, questionnaire design—as well as sampling and data analysis—was identified as one of the key areas in which RAND could most help the KRSO develop expertise. During the February 2012 visit of the RAND team to Erbil, the RAND and KRSO teams engaged in intensive discussions on the sampling and questionnaire. These discussions were motivated through two workshops led by RAND staff, one on sampling (discussed in the Chapter Two) and one on questionnaire design.

The questionnaire design workshop covered a range of issues that need to be considered when designing a survey, such as the format of questions, use of skip patterns, choosing appropriate recall periods for questions, and how to use field testing to improve the questionnaire design.[1] It went through correct practices and common mistakes in survey designs, and provided real-world examples. It also discussed how these principles would be followed in the context of the KRLFS.

Following this visit, RAND and KRSO staff worked together to design the questionnaire for the KRLFS. The discussion focused on a range of issues, among them how to ensure that both the questions and the response categories incorporated all relevant possibilities in the KRI context. Iterative reviews of different survey modules took place until a draft of the questionnaire was ready for translation and field testing.

[1] See Appendix F in the online companion volume for the workshop presentation.

Design of Previous Surveys and Information Gaps

Surveys carried out in the KRI or all of Iraq that contain information on employment include the IHSES (2007 and 2012), the Iraq Employment Survey (2008), and the Iraq Knowledge Network (IKN) survey (2011). While these provided valuable information, their design was not optimal for monitoring trends in unemployment and other labor market indicators. Other than the Iraq Employment Survey, these multipurpose surveys are too lengthy to be administered at frequent intervals. For example, the IHSES is a comprehensive general-purpose household survey that includes sections on housing, household expenditures, and health, among other nonlabor topics. This makes frequent administration of the IHSES impractical; indeed, the last two IHSES surveys took place five years apart. Therefore, to meet monitoring objectives, it was necessary to develop a smaller, more-focused labor survey that could easily be carried out at regular intervals.[2]

In assessing the need for, and content of, a new survey, we also closely examined the questions and definitions of key labor force concepts used in past surveys. The questions used to define work and unemployment are not completely consistent across these surveys and are not always precisely defined, which has contributed to differences in estimates for these indicators. For example, the 2008 Iraq Employment Survey asks about work in the last week but does not explicitly ask about unpaid work in family enterprises, which is part of the standard ILO definition of employment, as discussed below.

Further, it is important to account for the possibility that individuals work in more than one job, which is thought to be important in the KRI; the IHSES covers this well, but the other surveys do not. In addition, the earlier surveys generally do not provide enough information to adequately capture the distinction between formal and informal employment. The share of formal employment is an important marker of an economy's development, but addressing the distinction requires collecting information on a range of job-related characteristics.

In sum, our examination of previous surveys used in the KRI suggested the need for a focused, ongoing labor force survey that is consistent with international ILO standards for such surveys; would capture key labor force topics, such as formal and informal work; and would also capture the specific characteristics of the KRI's labor market.

Objectives of the Questionnaire Design

Based on the considerations noted above, the survey design was intended to meet three main objectives.

Provide Useful and Timely Data to Inform Policymaking

First and foremost, the survey was designed to meet the information needs of KRI policymakers. The most important need that key KRG officials expressed was to have accurate and up-to-date information on the unemployment rate in the KRI and in specific regions. Related standard indicators are the labor force participation rate and the employment rate (the difference between the two is the unemployment rate). Of course, the employment issues the KRI and other regions face go beyond these basic indicators: Policymakers are also concerned about the

[2] The IKN survey has been discontinued and therefore cannot provide periodic updates on the labor force situation.

type of employment in which the workforce is engaged, along various dimensions. Hence, there is interest in the distribution of the workforce across economic sectors, for example, industry and services; across occupations; across the private and public sectors; and across formal and informal work. A further clear area of interest is pay and benefits: how these differ across types of work and types of workers, for example, and how they are changing over time. Other potentially important labor-related factors that need to be understood are high levels of migration within the KRI (e.g., rural to urban migration), migration from outside the KRI, emigration for work, and underemployment of those who are working.

Since the KRLFS will be administered quarterly, it will provide information on *trends* in these measures, which is as important if not more so than information just on the levels of these indicators at one point in time. Thus policymakers will be able, for example, to use the survey to understand whether unemployment is increasing or decreasing (and among which areas or groups in the population it is changing). The survey can also be used to track shifts over time in, among other factors, the shares of employment in the public sector and in manufacturing and changes in women's participation in the labor market or in specific sectors.

Provide Internationally Comparable Information

It is very useful to be able to compare employment trends in the KRI with trends in the rest of Iraq, in other countries of the region, and globally. Among other things, this helps to disentangle Iraq-wide and global trends from phenomena specific to the KRI. Achieving this objective requires carefully designing a questionnaire to yield measures—of work, participation, sector, etc.—that are comparable to those other surveys collect internationally, whenever possible. This is not a trivial concern, since seemingly small modifications in the way a question is asked or the way an indicator is calculated can lead to significantly different estimates. Much if not most labor force statistics reporting around the world follows ILO guidelines for calculating the unemployment rate and other statistics, leading countries to use survey questionnaires with similar structure and questions. However, there is some scope for adapting the questions to the needs of particular contexts.

Similarly, economic activities by sector are usually classified using the United Nation's International Standard Industrial Classification of All Economic Activities, and occupations are classified according to the International Standard Classification of Occupations (ISCO)—both also either ILO initiated or supported. The KRLFS design adheres closely to these conventions.

We also examined a range of existing labor force surveys from the region—including the Iraq employment survey and surveys from Jordan, Palestine, Bahrain, and Turkey—as well as surveys from Canada, the United States, and many other countries. It should be emphasized that the process of designing the survey structure and questions for the KRLFS was not simply a matter of merely using questions from other surveys. RAND and the KRSO worked closely to ensure that questions and response categories were appropriate for the KRI context, with respect to wording and other factors, while adhering to international guidelines.

Achieve the Above Objectives While Keeping the Respondent Burden Reasonable

Respondent burden refers to how long it takes to complete an interview. It is crucial to the success of a survey because having a very long questionnaire usually means a higher refusal rate. This leads to what is known as *nonresponse bias*: Since those who do agree to be in the survey may not be representative of the overall population, the resulting estimates will not accurately reflect the characteristics of the population as a whole. This can also result in lower-quality responses because of respondent fatigue (response bias). For the KRLFS, these considerations are especially important because it is a panel survey, in which the same households are interviewed over multiple survey rounds. An excessively long interview in the first round may cause many respondents to refuse to participate in later rounds, resulting in unacceptable levels of attrition.

Discussions with the KRSO and on international experience suggested that an interview lasting about 30 to 45 minutes constituted a maximum burden, and the survey was designed accordingly (field testing and the actual implementation confirmed that this objective was met). The trade-off is that a relatively short survey instrument limits the amount of information that can be included in the survey. Therefore, the design team had to carefully choose the most important components for inclusion in the survey. Going forward, there is flexibility to add a small number of additional questions to capture important topics or policy issues that may emerge.

Structure of the KRLFS Questionnaire

Like most household surveys, the questionnaire is arranged in a series of modules covering different topics, after an initial introductory information page to record basic information about the household and survey administration details. Below we describe each briefly in turn and discuss some key variables in each.[3]

Introductory Information

The introductory section collects data on the geographic location of the household visited including Global Positioning System (GPS) coordinates, date of visit, and interview result (whether it was completed or could not be completed for some reason). This section is important for tracking respondents. In each round of the survey, one-half of the respondents from the previous round are recontacted and interviewed, so accurate information on location of the household is essential.

Household Roster

The roster records basic information on all household members: age, sex, relation to household head, and marital status if over age 12. Since households are interviewed in multiple rounds, the roster asks if any members from the previous round are no longer living in the household and if any new members have been added, whether by birth or joining from other households. Questions are asked about migration: where household members were born and where they lived in 2003. Other questions cover the destination and reason for moving of members who have left the household since the last interview. Hence, the module is designed to capture the dynamic situation of the KRI with respect to both in- and outmigration, which can be both a reflection and determinant of local labor market conditions.

[3] See Appendix C in the online companion volume for full questionnaire.

Education

This short module gathers basic information on the schooling of all household members age 5 and older. This information will enable analysis of the various labor force indicators by education level (for example, unemployment rate of secondary versus university graduates). It will also permit the tracking of changes in the skills of the labor over time.

Labor Force Participation

For household members 12 and older, this section establishes whether the individual has any current work activity. As discussed in Chapter Five, work is defined, in accordance to international guidelines and practice, to include paid labor, self-employment, and unpaid labor on family famers or businesses. These and other questions closely follow ILO guidelines and formats used in other labor force surveys around the world.

Nonworking Cases

Respondents who indicated they have not worked in the last week and have no activity to which they will return are given this module. It asks questions about availability for and willingness to work and about job search activities. The questions are again consistent with ILO guidelines and standard international practice. They are used to determine whether an individual is to be counted as participating in the labor force, as employed, or as unemployed, as detailed in Chapter Five.

Working Cases

Individuals who are determined in the labor force participation module to be working are given this module. This module gathers detailed information on up to two activities and summary information on any additional activities (which proved to be very rare in the first round of the survey). Hence, the questionnaire accommodates multiple job holding. For each of the first two jobs, information is gathered on economic sector, occupation using ISCO codes, and "ownership sector" (government, state enterprise, self-employment, etc.). This enables tracking of trends in employment in the KRI in different industries or by public versus private employment, for example. We use the two-digit level of the most recent ISCO.

The module also collects information on the nature of the workplace (including location and number of employees) and on whether the employer provides various job benefits, such as sick leave and vacation. These benefits are important nonwage measures of job quality, and both the benefit information and workplace characteristics can be used to categorize a job as formal or informal, according to different definitions. Finally, respondents are asked about their hours of work and earnings in the job, which will allow comparison of pay across governorates or other locations, job type or sector, education, and gender and allow measurement of the extent of part time and underemployment.

Part-Time Work and Underemployment

To capture information on part-time work and underemployment, this section confirms the total hours worked per week reported in earlier parts of the survey. Since workers may have multiple activities, this question measures the combined hours in all activities. It also asks respondents if they would prefer to work more than they currently do and, if so, whether they are trying to find additional work. As discussed in Chapter Five, these questions can be used to calculate the shares of individuals who are part-time workers and who are underemployed.

Summary

Existing surveys that cover KRI employment issues suffered from gaps, which highlighted the benefits of instituting the routine collection of a focused labor force survey to inform policymaking. We therefore worked with the KRSO to design a questionnaire to gather reliable and frequent information on unemployment and other factors in a way that is internationally comparable, while accounting for the realities of the KRI labor market and economy and not overburdening survey respondents.

CHAPTER FOUR

Data Collection, Cleaning, and Validation

Data Collection Process for the KRLFS

Reflecting the KRSO's established expertise in survey fieldwork implementation, the KRSO staff, led by the central office in Erbil and with support from each of the three governorate offices, implemented the KRLFS. RAND supported the data collection process through a set of preimplementation workshops (summarized later in this section) and by making staff available to help the KRSO address issues as they arose. The KRSO carried out the following steps:

- A field test of the survey on a small sample of households in one rural and one urban cluster took place in June 2012. The KRSO and RAND discussed the results and made numerous (mostly relatively minor) changes to the questionnaire. In addition to assessing the survey questionnaire, the field test was also an opportunity to test and refine fieldwork procedures.
- Once the questionnaire was revised, KRSO staff devised and carried out the training of enumerators (survey interviewers) in sessions held at each regional office.
- The main KRLFS data collection took place during July 2012, with the KRSO managing the supervisors and teams of enumerators.

KRSO staff conducted the fieldwork autonomously. Both the training and fieldwork went smoothly, reflecting the staff's experience in data collection. The KRSO managed the process and resolved issues and obstacles and needed little assistance from RAND.

Data Cleaning and Validation[1]

Completed KRLFS survey forms were transmitted to the three governorate offices for data entry, and the electronic data were then transferred to the central KRSO office in Erbil. KRSO staff compiled the final data set for use in analysis.

The KRSO and RAND conducted separate, parallel data cleaning and assessment processes. This ensured accuracy and provided KRSO staff the opportunity to start the data analysis process independently.

Through the parallel data checks, both RAND and the KRSO identified some relatively minor problems in the survey and data collection. The fact that both teams independently

[1] In Berry et al., 2012, Chapter Six, we laid out, in general terms, the practical steps involved in high-quality data collection and management.

reached the same conclusions indicated that these problems were limited and in no way compromised the integrity of the data. Among the problems found were the following:

- Some individuals who were determined to be *not employed* were still asked how many hours they worked. In this case, it was necessary to recode the hours worked as *missing*.
- In some cases, interviewers used a code for nonresponse that was different from the one specified in the survey.
- For a few observations in the sample, responses to particular questions were not consistent with other responses. For example, the introduction question asked for the number of children aged 5–17, but the roster data would suggest a different number of children in the household.

RAND and the KRSO discussed these issues, which led to minor refinements of the questionnaire for the second-round KRLFS (completed in late 2012) and to adjustments in the training procedures for future survey rounds.

Workshops and Capacity Building

In preparation for the KRLFS implementation, RAND conducted two workshops with the KRSO that focused on data collection and data cleaning and management processes:

- The Data Collection and Entry workshop was conducted in May 2012.[2] The goal of this workshop was to review best practices and potential challenges related to the data collection process. Specifically, the workshop focused on:
  - survey preparation
  - the process of preparing to collect data
  - survey implementation
  - data entry and verification
- The Overview of Data Processing workshop was also conducted in May 2012.[3] This workshop focused on the process of managing and using data:
  - data management and information protection (e.g., ensuring confidentiality)
  - effective data cleaning practices, checking for and correcting inconsistencies and other errors, and determining when to correct the raw data and when not to do so
  - proper file directory structures for organizing data
  - program documentation.

Each workshop was attended by approximately ten KRSO staff from both the central and governorate offices and lasted approximately two days. Following the workshops, the RAND and KRSO teams communicated closely as the data entry and cleaning progressed.

---

[2] See Appendix G in the online companion volume for the workshop presentation.

[3] See Appendix H in the online companion volume for the workshop presentation.

Summary

The data collection component of the project was critical for producing a high-quality data set for the first round of the KRLFS. RAND supported this process through workshops on data collection and data cleaning and management. The RAND team also provided support to the KRSO team throughout the data collection process, but the KRSO managed the process independently and successfully.

CHAPTER FIVE

Analysis and Results

Outline of the KRLFS Analysis Process

The KRSO and RAND jointly conducted the data analysis for the 2012 KRLFS, a process designed to facilitate timely reporting of results and capacity building within the KRSO. Once data collection was complete, the KRSO provided RAND with complete, final copies of the KRLFS dataset. Working from the discussions on questionnaire design and critical labor force statistics, the RAND team developed a set of labor force indicators (reported in the next subsection) and provided the KRSO team with the metrics and guidance on how to construct these indicators from survey items. The two teams then worked in parallel to construct the critical labor force statistics. During RAND's October 2012 trip to the KRI, the RAND and KRSO teams consulted over multiple meetings to compare their respective analyses and results. In an ongoing process, RAND is working with KRSO staff to refine their analytical work and the reporting of results.

The next section presents the main labor force findings RAND compiled from the 2012 KRLFS and provides a basis for long-term KRSO analysis and reporting. The purpose of this presentation is to discuss and—where possible—explain key patterns. However, a more-comprehensive analysis of the KRI labor market and of specific aspects of it is beyond the scope of this report and is left for future research.

Main Results from KRLFS

This section presents labor force indicators for the KRI based on the quarterly KRLFS and compares these indicators with those for several other countries. The results presented here are from the survey KRSO conducted in the third quarter of 2012 (specifically, July 2012). As discussed in Chapters Two and Three, the KRLFS is designed to provide consistent and up-to-date information on a range of labor force indicators for the KRI.

Each of the following subsections first precisely defines the indicator of interest, then presents the findings for it. For the main indicators, we present the ME in parentheses following the indicator number. As discussed in Chapter Two, the ME is a measure of the precision or reliability of an estimate from a sample. For example, if the estimated unemployment rate is 6 percent with a 2-percent ME, we can say with 95-percent certainty that the actual unemployment rate falls between 4 and 8 percent, that is, within plus or minus 2 percentage points of our estimate. The larger the sample, all things equal, the smaller the ME, the more reliable the estimates. As noted in Chapter Two, the KRLFS has been designed to have reasonably precise estimates (low MEs) or better for key indicators for the all-KRI sample and subgroup analysis.

Labor Force Participation

The *labor force* is defined as the total number of individuals 15 years and older who are "economically active," meaning that they are currently working or are not working but are available and actively searching for work. *Work* is defined, following international conventions, to include having a wage job or to be working on one's own, in a family business, or on a farm, whether directly for pay or not. It is international practice to classify as working or *employed* those who worked for at least one hour in the week preceding the interview date. The percentage of the working age population that is in the labor force is the *labor force participation rate* (see Figure 5.1).

The KRLFS data show that the KRI labor force in the third quarter of 2012 constituted 38.4 percent (ME ±0.72 percent)[1] of the total population aged 15 years and older—a relatively

Figure 5.1
Labor Force Status of the KRI Population and Definitions of Terms

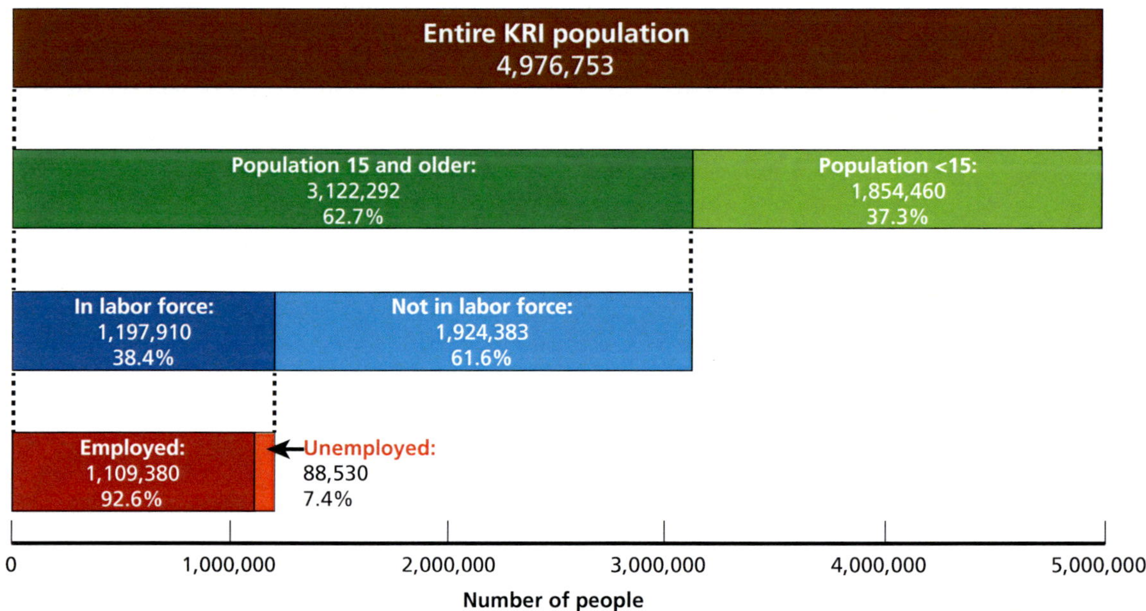

SOURCE: KRLFS.
NOTES: *In labor force* includes both the employed and the unemployed. The labor force participation rate is the number in the labor force divided by the population 15 and older. The unemployment rate is the number unemployed divided by the number in the labor force. The employed-to-population ratio is the number employed divided by the population 15 and older. The unemployment to population ratio is the number unemployed divided by the population 15 and older.
RAND *RR293-5.1*

---

[1] In this case, the ME is plus or minus 0.72 percentage points (less than 1 percent) around the mean of 38.4 percent.

low rate.[2] Although this rate is essentially the same as in Jordan (38 percent), it is significantly lower than in Turkey (approximately 50 percent) and Egypt (approximately 48 percent). The low overall participation rate in the KRI is largely driven by the very low participation of women. Indeed, men greatly outnumbered women in the labor force. Among men aged 15 and older, about two-thirds, or 65.7 percent (±1.2 percent), were in the labor force, while only 12.2 percent (±1.0 percent) of women were in the labor force. However, among male youth (aged 15–24), only 37.8 percent (±2.2 percent) were in the labor force, largely because many were still studying. For female youth, the participation rate was only 6.1 percent (±1.2 percent).

Employment Rate, Unemployment, and Underemployment

The labor force comprises two groups of individuals: those who are working (i.e., employed) and those who are not working but are willing and available to work and are also searching for work (the unemployed). In the KRI in the third quarter of 2012, 92.6 percent of the labor force was employed, whether full or part time. This group comprised 35.5 percent of the total KRI population age 15 years and older; this is the *employment-population ratio.*

The share of the labor force that is unemployed is called the *unemployment rate* (see Figure 5.1 for definitions). The unemployment rate is a central indicator of how well the labor market, and the economy as a whole, is functioning. High unemployment means that an economy is not generating enough jobs to absorb all individuals who are willing and able to contribute to economic output.

The overall unemployment rate in the KRI was 7.4 percent (±0.93 percent). While this is not low, the situation in the KRI nonetheless compares favorably to most countries in the region. For example, in 2012, Turkey had an unemployment rate of 8.4 percent, while Egypt had an unemployment rate of 12.6 percent. In Jordan and Syria (in 2011), unemployment was 11 percent and 14.9 percent, respectively (Figure 5.2).[3] The KRI unemployment rate is also lower than the latest available measure for the rest of Iraq, from the 2011 IKN survey, which indicates 8.6 percent unemployment in the rest of Iraq.[4] The *unemployment-population ratio*—the percentage of the total population 15 and older (not just the labor force) that is unemployed—is also sometimes of interest; this figure is 2.8 percent for the KRI.

Unemployment Rate by Age, Gender, and Education

The unemployment rate for a particular subset of the population equals the number of unemployed people in that group divided by the number in the labor force from that group. The

---

[2] In this and all subsequent calculations from the KRLFS, weights are used to adjust for the sampling design and nonresponse.

[3] As noted in the International Monetary Fund metadata, Turkey, Egypt, and Syria all have unemployment definitions similar to those KRLFS uses. These refer to individuals who are (1) not working, (2) available to work, and (3) actively seeking work (International Monetary Fund, "Dissemination Standards Bulletin Board," website, 2012). Further, these countries also consider those who say they have found work but have not yet started to be unemployed. However, the reference periods for seeking work are different. According to the ILO, in Egypt it is the last three months, while in Turkey it is the last four weeks, and in Syria it is unclear. The KRLFS uses a reference period of 7 days. The data for other countries are from their respective statistical organization—Turkey from TURKSTAT (Turkish Statistical Institute, website, undated), Egypt from Central Agency for Public Mobilization and Statistics, website, 2013; and Syria from CBSSYR.

[4] For the KRI, the IKN indicates an unemployment rate of 6 percent, somewhat lower than the 7.4 percent we estimated from the KRLFS. Given differences in sample and timing between the two surveys, this relatively modest difference is not unexpected. Hence, the IKN alone suggests an even larger gap (the difference between 6 and 8.7 percent) between the KRI and the rest of Iraq than the comparison in the figure implies.

Figure 5.2
Unemployment Rate for the KRI and Other Economies

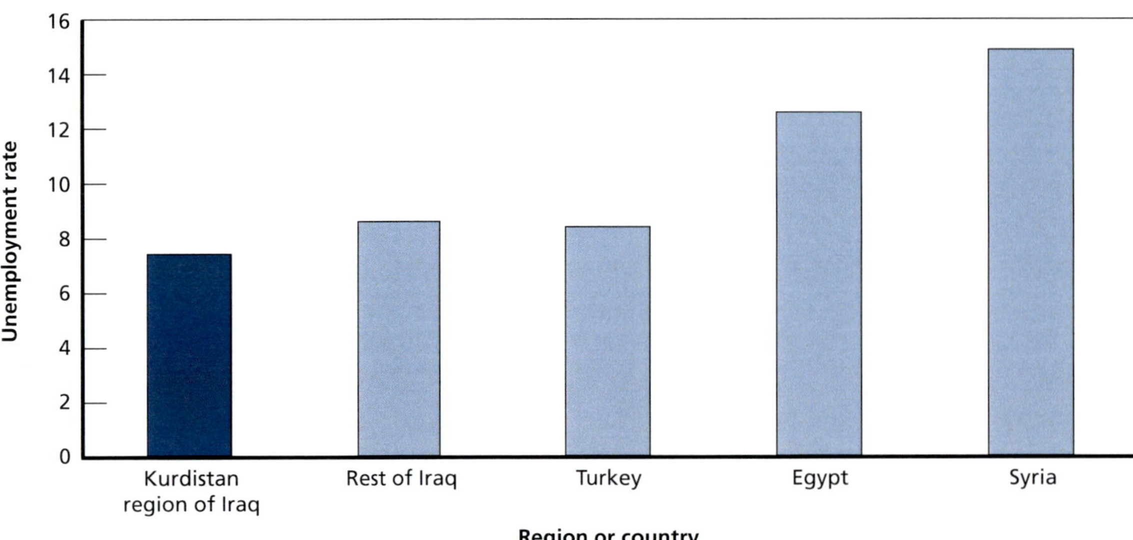

SOURCE: KRLFS for the KRI, ILO for Turkey, Central Agency for Public Mobilization and Statistics, website, 2013, for Egypt, and CBSSYR for Syria. Data for Turkey and Egypt are for the second quarter of 2012; data for Syria and the rest of Iraq are for 2011; and KRI data are from the third quarter of 2012.
RAND *RR293-5.2*

unemployment rates for youth in particular are closely watched because this indicates whether the economy is generating economic opportunities for this group, thereby aiding both economic growth and social stability.

Within the KRI, youth unemployment (ages 15–24) is 17.6 percent, significantly higher than the 7.4 percent rate for the entire labor force. The phenomenon of high youth unemployment is well known in the Middle East. However, as with unemployment overall, youth unemployment in the KRI is among the lowest in the region. The unemployment rate for the 15 to 24 age group dropped in the second quarter of 2012 to 16.1 percent in Turkey but was 35.8 percent in Syria and 28 percent in Jordan. The unemployment rate in Egypt for those ages 20–24 was 41.4 percent in 2012 (this rate, however, is partially a reflection of the effects of the 2011 revolution on the economy).[5]

While youth unemployment in the KRI is somewhat less serious than in many countries of the region, it is still a concern for policy. As in other countries, the reasons may be a combination of poor job skills even among educated youth, unrealistic expectations about employment opportunities, and/or an unwillingness to work outside the public sector or formal sector despite limited available positions. The causes and possible solutions to high youth unemployment in the KRI merit further attention.

Further, gender differences in youth unemployment are noteworthy. In the KRI, the unemployment rate for female youth is much higher, at 48.9 percent, compared to 12.8 percent for young men (Figure 5.3). Despite the higher unemployment rate for young women, however, the actual number of unemployed young men is higher than the number of unemployed

---

[5] Data for the full 15–24 age group are unavailable for Egypt. Data for Turkey and Egypt are for the second quarter of 2012, while those for Syria are for 2011. Note that Turkey recently experienced a sharp decline in unemployment rates for youth within one quarter, falling from 10.2 percent in the first quarter of 2012 to 8.4 percent in the second quarter of 2012.

Figure 5.3
Unemployment Rate by Age Group and Gender

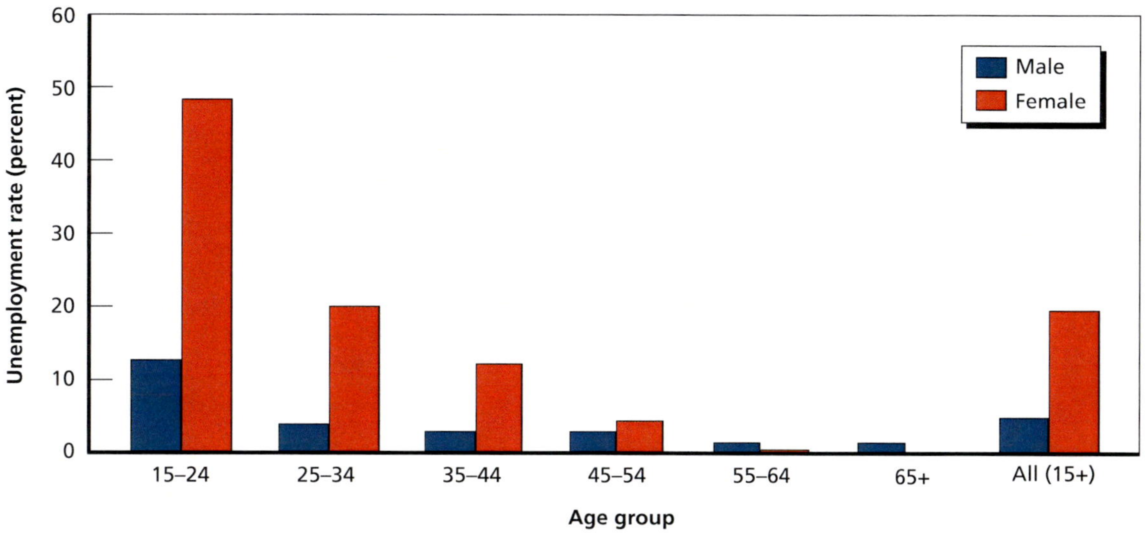

SOURCE: KRLFS.
RAND *RR293-5.3*

young women because many fewer young women are in the labor force. For older age groups, unemployment is significantly lower for both men and women but is still generally much higher for women than men. For example, the unemployment rate for those aged 25 to 34 is 20.2 percent for females but 3.8 percent for males.

As shown in Figure 5.3, the lowest unemployment rate is for those aged 55 to 64, for whom it is 1.5 percent overall and similar for both genders.

The higher unemployment rates for women, particularly young women, suggests that females entering the workforce face difficulties in getting hired. Further, the low participation rate of young women (and women overall) noted earlier may also be evidence of such difficulties, if many women do not enter or stay in the labor force because of difficulties in finding work.

Finally, Table 5.1 considers patterns by rural or urban location and education level. Labor force participation and unemployment rates are both higher in urban areas but modestly so.

Table 5.1
Labor Force Participation and Unemployment, by Area and Education, Age 15+

	Labor Force Participation (%)	Unemployment (%)
Rural areas	35.3	6.0
Urban areas	39.0	7.7
Primary education	53.6	6.9
Secondary education	41.3	8.5
College degree	80.3	10.9

SOURCE: KRLFS.

Participation is very high for those with college degrees (80 percent) and substantially lower for those with less education, especially secondary completers (41 percent). This is due in part to the fact that some individuals at the younger end of the age range considered (which starts at 15) whose highest degree is primary or secondary are in fact still attending school at the next level and not yet in the labor force.

Unemployment rates are also higher among those who are better educated. One factor behind this pattern is likely to be that those with more education tend to hold out for specific kinds of highly skilled jobs and have more family resources to support them while searching for work.

Number of Unemployed by Age Group and Gender

In addition to the unemployment rate, it is useful to examine the actual *number* of people who are unemployed. For example, we have already noted that, while unemployment is high among young women, a greater number of young men than women are unemployed; approximately 60 percent of unemployed youth are male (Figure 5.4). As indicated above, this reflects the fact that relatively few young women are in the labor force to begin with. As Figure 5.4 shows, for most age groups, the number of males unemployed exceeds females unemployed, despite a higher rate of unemployment for women.

The largest group of unemployed people in the KRI is young men aged 15 to 24 (24,838), followed by young women aged 15 to 24 (14,683) and women aged 25 to 34 (16,232).

Labor Force Indicators by Governorate

Labor force indicators vary markedly by governorate. As Figure 5.5 shows, a larger proportion of individuals age 15+ are part of the labor force (that is, economically active) in Sulaymaniya (41.9 percent) than in Erbil (36.7 percent) or Duhok (34.7 percent). The highest unemployment rate is in Sulaymaniya (8.6 percent), followed by Duhok (6.8 percent) and Erbil (6.2 per-

Figure 5.4
Total Number of Unemployed by Age Group and Gender

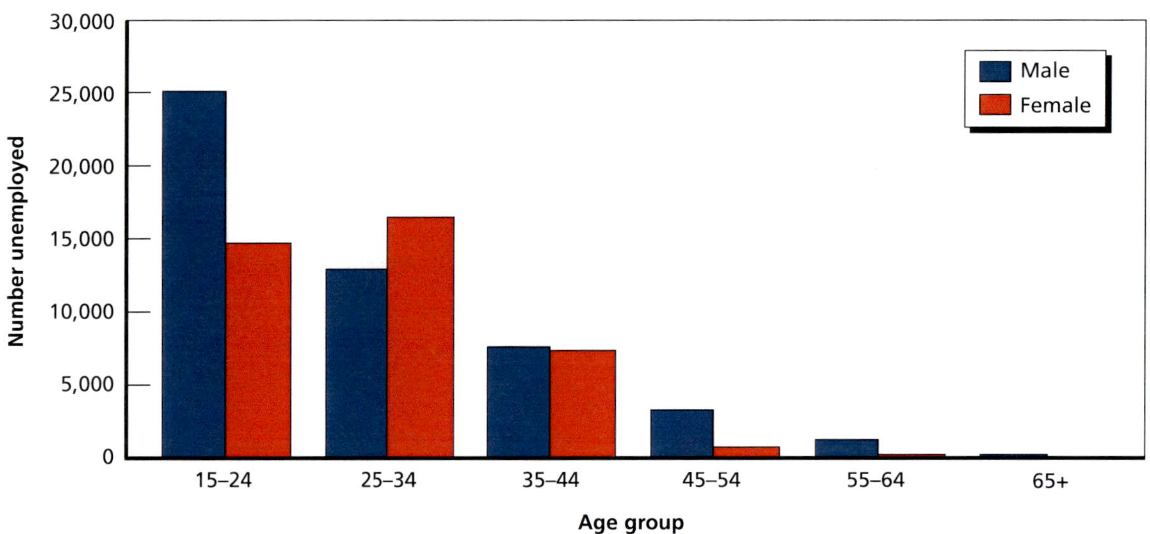

SOURCE: KRLFS.
RAND *RR293-5.4*

Figure 5.5
Labor Force Indicators for Governorates of the KRI and Other Economies

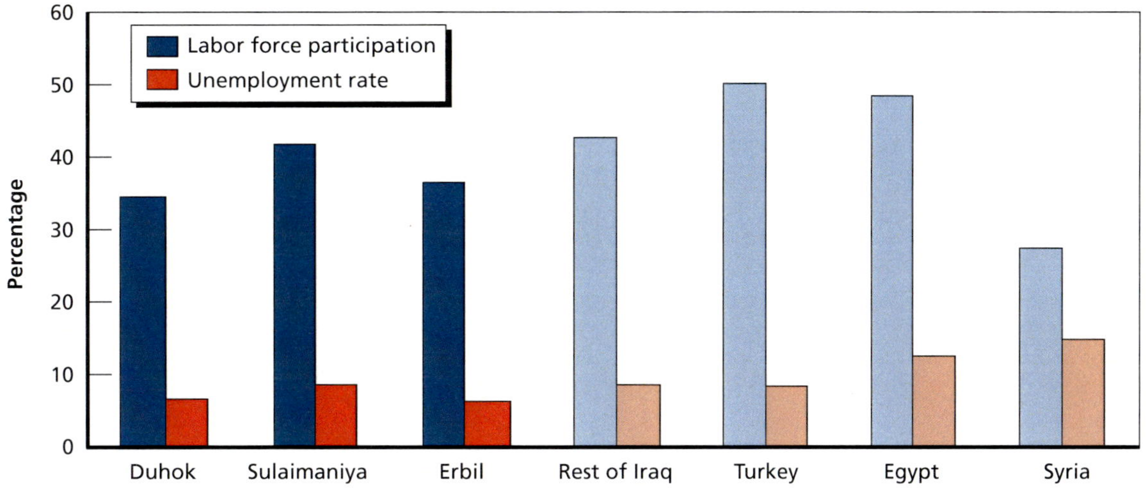

SOURCES: KRLFS for the KRI governorates; IKN for the rest of Iraq; ILO for Turkey; Central Agency for Public Mobilization and Statistics, website, 2013 for Egypt; and CBSSYR for Syria. Data for Turkey and Egypt are for the second quarter of 2012; data for Syria and the Rest of Iraq are for 2011; and KRI data are from third quarter 2012.
RAND *RR293-5.5*

cent). Therefore, Sulaymaniya has the highest labor force participation rate but also the highest unemployment rate.

Table 5.2 considers governorate patterns further by distinguishing male and female participation and unemployment rates. Interestingly, both male and female participation appear to be higher in Sulaymaniya than elsewhere. For example, 16 percent of women over age 15 are in the labor force in Sulaymaniya, compared with 7 percent and 11 percent in Duhok and Erbil, respectively. This difference explains a significant part of the higher overall (male plus female) participation rate in Sulaymaniya noted above, with the somewhat higher male participation in Sulaymaniya explaining the rest. Higher female participation in Sulaymaniya also explains, in part, the higher overall unemployment rate for that governorate. Since women have a much higher unemployment rate than men, having a relatively large proportion of women in the labor force means that the overall (male plus female) unemployment rate will be

Table 5.2
Labor Force Participation and Unemployment, by Governorate and Gender, Age 15+

Governorate	Gender	Labor Force Participation (%)	Unemployment (%)
Duhok	Male	63.31	6.51
	Female	7.06	9.20
Sulaymaniya	Male	68.76	5.23
	Female	16.10	22.32
Erbil	Male	64.01	3.61
	Female	11.22	20.29

higher, all things equal. Even in Sulaymaniya, however, female participation, at 16 percent, is still extremely low.

Labor Force Indicators by District

The data also suggest notable differences by district in these indicators (see Figures 5.6 and 5.7). The estimated labor force participation rate ranges between 26.9 percent in the district of Soran in Erbil governorate to 47.4 percent in the district of Sharbajer in Sulaymaniya governorate (the KRI-wide figure is 38.4 percent). However, drawing inferences about such district-level variation requires some caution because the district figures involve relatively small samples so are somewhat imprecise. The MEs for these estimates range from 2 percent to 7.8 percent, with

Figure 5.6
Labor Force Participation by District

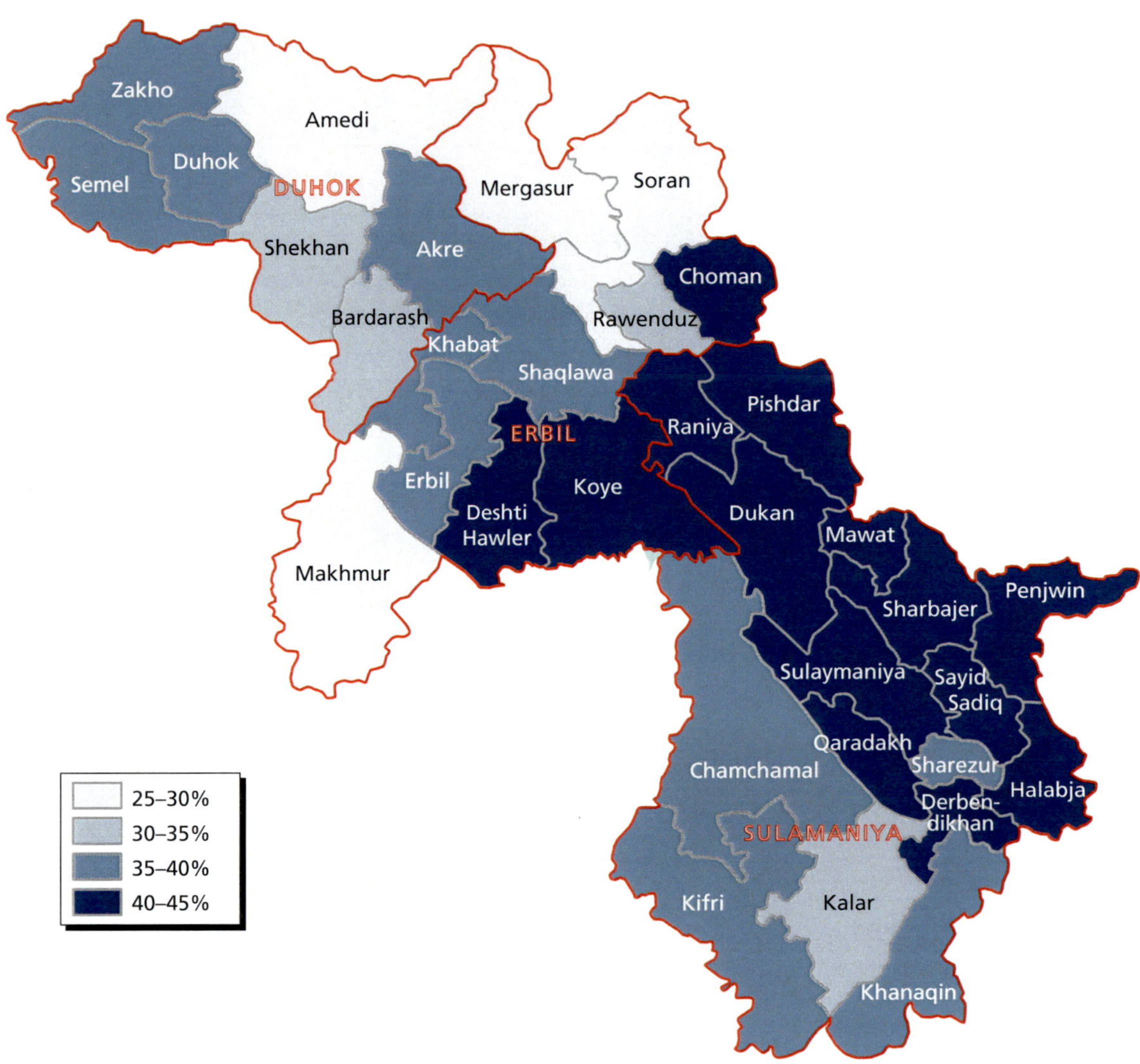

SOURCE: KRLFS.
RAND *RR293-5.6*

Figure 5.7
Unemployment by District

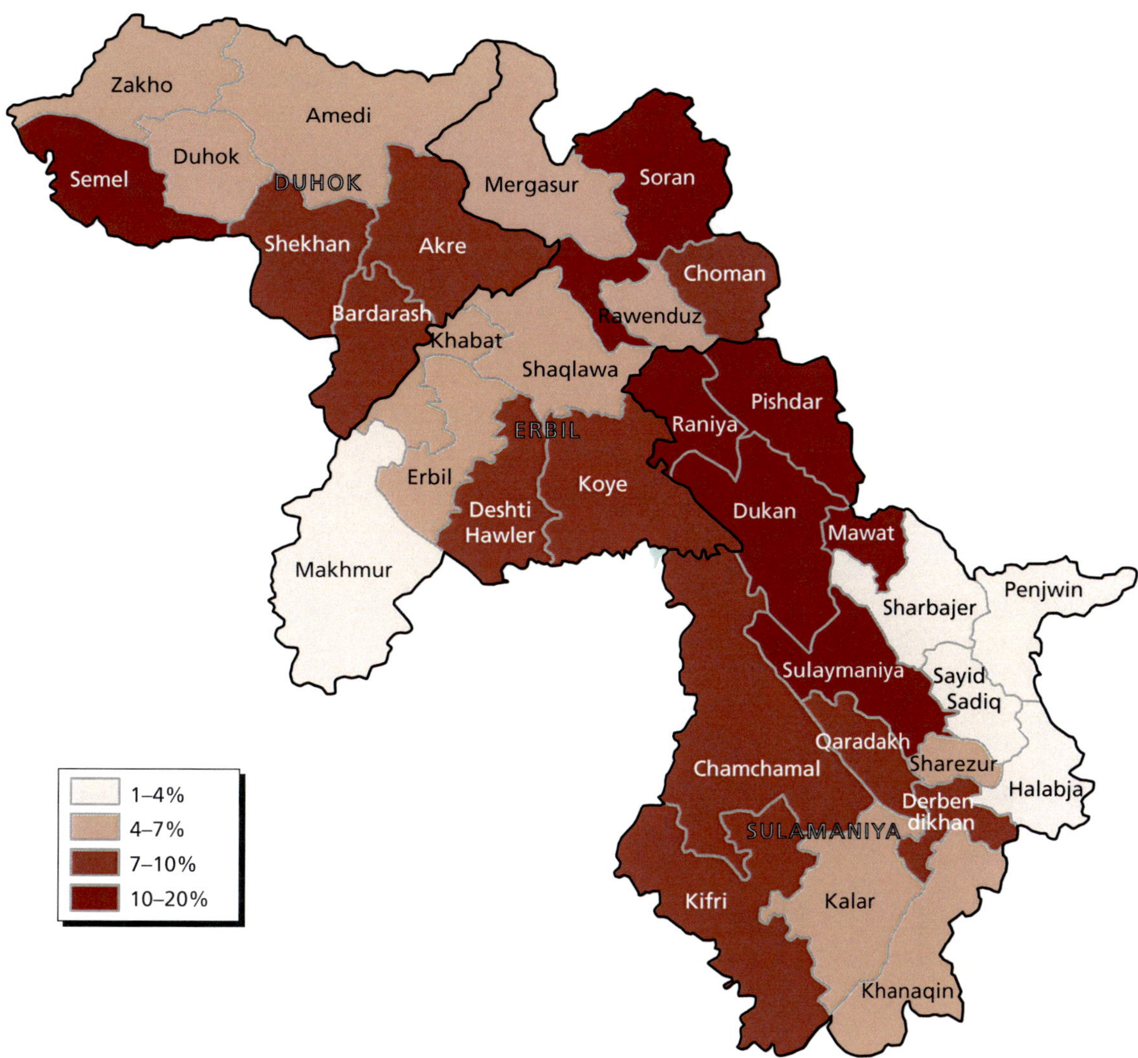

SOURCE: KRLFS.
RAND *RR293-5.7*

a mean of 4 percent. Hence, on average, we can only be certain that the true participation rate is between 4 percent below and 4 percent above the estimated rate.[6]

Figure 5.7 shows the unemployment rate by district. This ranges from less than 1 percent for Sayid Sadiq district in Sulaymaniya governorate to 19.2 percent for Dukan, also in Sulaymaniya (the KRI-wide average is 7.4 percent). District-level unemployment appears to be the most variable in Sulaymaniya (which includes the district with the lowest unemployment rate and the one with the highest), which, as mentioned previously, is also the governorate with the highest overall unemployment rate (Figure 5.4). While these data suggest substantial unemployment variability across districts, this observation is also based on small samples and thus requires caution. The margins of error range from 1.5 percent to 7 percent with an aver-

[6] This will vary by district because the MEs are different for each district.

age of 4.3 percent. So, as with participation rates, we can only be certain that, on average, the true unemployment rate is between 4 percent below and 4 percent above the estimated rate. It appears that districts with very low unemployment (the four districts with unemployment under 4 percent) are more rural and agricultural than the rest. Beyond that, there are no clear patterns in district-level unemployment with respect to rural population share and share agriculturally employed.

Full-Time and Part-Time Employment and Underemployment

The definition of *full-time* work depends on the context of a particular country or region. Here, we consider full time to be at least 35 hours per week, based on standard government work schedules in the KRI. Overall, taking into account hours worked across all jobs for an individual, 76.5 percent of all those who work (which, it should be reiterated, includes any type of work, not just wage work) worked at least 35 hours per week; 11.1 percent worked between 30 and 34 hours; and 12.5 percent worked fewer than 30 hours (Figure 5.8).

Therefore, nearly one-quarter (23.5 percent) of all those employed (including those self-employed) worked fewer than 35 hours per week, that is, worked part time according to our definition. The percentage working part time is substantially smaller for men than for women, who presumably are more likely to work part time to balance time in the labor market with household work or child care: 40.6 percent of women employees worked fewer than 35 hours compared to only 20.7 percent for men.

As Table 5.3 shows, the share of employed who worked full time is the largest in Sulaymaniya governorate, where only 14.6 percent of the employed population worked less than 35 hours, and only 13.7 percent worked less than 30 hours, compared with 23.5 percent and 18.6 percent, respectively, for the KRI overall. This is consistent with the higher rate of labor force participation for Sulaymaniya, since both overall participation and a high degree of full-time employment for those who work are indicators of greater labor force involvement.

Figure 5.8
Percentage of Employed by Total Hours Worked

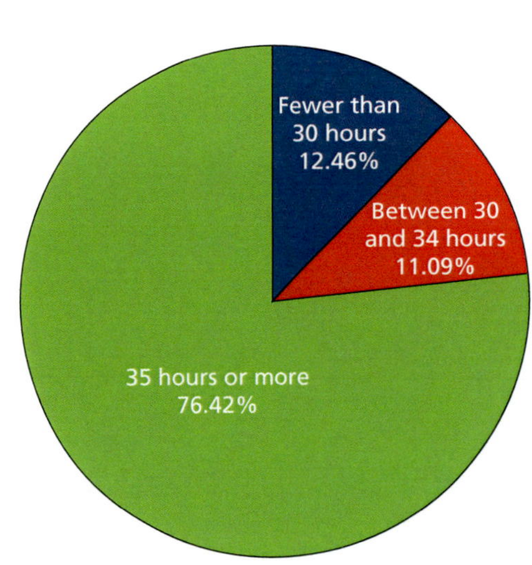

SOURCE: KRLFS.

RAND *RR293-5.8*

Table 5.3
Part-Time Employment as a Share of Total Employed Population, by Governorate

	Works fewer than 35 hours per week			Works fewer than 30 hours per week		
	Females	Males	Total	Females	Males	Total
All KRI	40.6	20.7	23.5	21.9	10.9	12.5
Erbil	68.6	24.6	30.5	37.5	10.2	13.9
Duhok	65.8	26.6	30.6	23.4	15.2	16.0
Sulaymaniya	15.0	14.5	14.6	11.4	9.2	9.6

SOURCE: KRLFS.

Overall for the KRI, then, a sizable portion of those who do work are working less than full time. Extensive part-time employment could signal that many individuals are unable to work as much as they would like and thus are being underutilized by the economy. Individuals who are employed less than full time because they cannot find more work are considered *underemployed*. On the other hand, part-time work no doubt reflects individual preferences to work less in many cases, especially for women, who often need to balance work and family responsibilities, as already noted.

To address this distinction, the KRLFS asked all employed individuals whether they *wanted* to work more than their current hours and whether they were actively seeking additional work. Formally, an individual is considered underemployed if he or she worked less than full time, was willing and able to work additional hours, and was looking for more work; hence, the definition is analogous to the standard definition for unemployment.

Considering first just the numbers who say they would like to work more, about 17 percent of those who worked less than 20 hours indicated they would like to work more hours (results not shown). Note that this group makes up only about 4 percent of all the employed and less than 20 percent of all part-time workers (those working less than 35 hours per week). Among those working between 21 and 35 hours (about 80 percent of all part time workers), 12.7 percent indicated that they would like to work more. This relatively small share is very similar to those for full-time workers saying they would like to work more. Finally, the data show that less than 10 percent of part-time employed both want to work more *and* are searching for more work, i.e., can be technically classified as underemployed. All in all, then, underemployment does not appear to be a significant phenomenon in the KRI; most of those working less than 35 hours per week do so willingly.

Formal and Informal Employment

In contrast to the definitions for labor force, employment, and unemployment, there is less consistency internationally in the way formality of employment is calculated from surveys. The KRLFS asks a series of questions that are used to determine whether a job is formal or informal. Following what is probably the most common practice, we consider jobs to be formal if they provide one or more standard benefits or feature an employment contract. Specifically, an employee is categorized as formal if he received any benefit (health insurance, paid vacation, or paid sick leave or if the employer contributes to the Social Guarantee Fund) or if he signed a contract for the job. If these conditions are not met, the employee's position is classified as informal. All self-employment or work in family enterprises or farms (which does not provide benefits or pay into the Social Guarantee Fund) is considered to be informal employment.

By this definition, slightly over one-half of all employment in the KRI (51.4 percent) can be characterized as formal, as shown in Figure 5.9. The formal share varies by governorate, with the highest in Erbil (54.8 percent) and the lowest in Duhok (46.6 percent). Such a prominent role for informal employment is characteristic of countries in the region. A recent study estimates that the average share of informal-sector employment is 67 percent for all Middle East and North African region countries.[7]

It is noteworthy that the vast majority—91 percent—of jobs defined as formal in the KRI are in the public sector. This confirms that the formal private sector of the KRI economy remains undeveloped.

There are also striking differences by gender. Women are much less likely to be found in informal employment than are men. As shown in Figure 5.10, 82.1 percent of employed women were formally employed (almost all in the public sector), while only 46.4 percent of employed men were in formal employment. This is in contrast to the situation in many economies, in which informal work, especially self-employment, offers women flexibility to combine work and family responsibilities. However, the data for the KRI suggest that private informal opportunities are few for women. An alternative (or additional) interpretation is that, for cultural reasons, women or their families do not consider private-sector work, especially informal-sector work, appropriate for them.

Figure 5.9
Formal and Informal Employment for Employed Individuals 15+

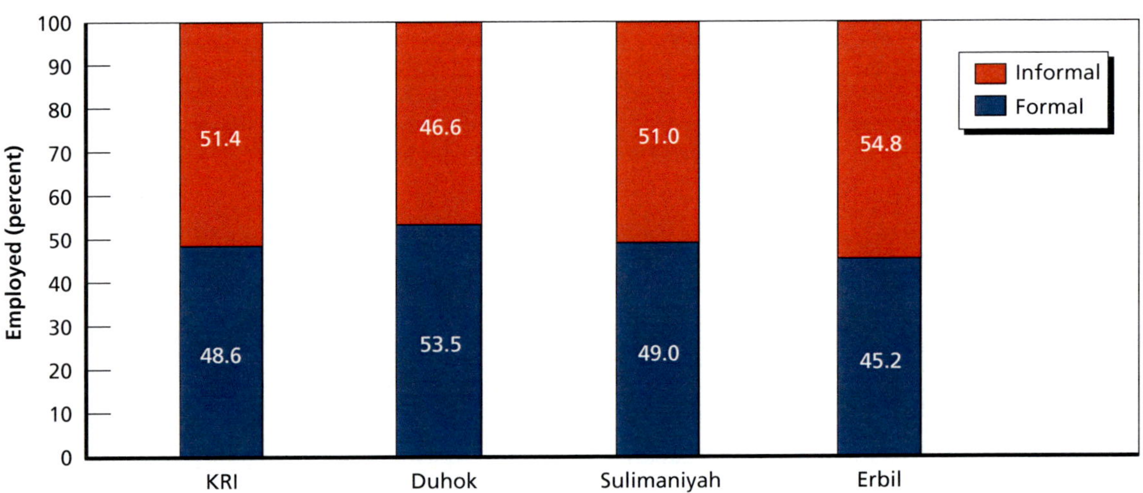

SOURCE: KRLFS.
RAND *RR293-5.9*

[7] Diego F. Angel-Urdinola and Kimie Tanabe, "Micro-Determinants of Informal Employment in the Middle East and North Africa Region," Washington, D.C.: World Bank Social, January 2012. It should be noted that these authors count jobs as formal only if the worker receives some form of pension benefit; this criterion is somewhat more restrictive than ours and so would tend to estimate a higher share of workers in informal employment.

Figure 5.10
Formal and Informal Employment by Gender

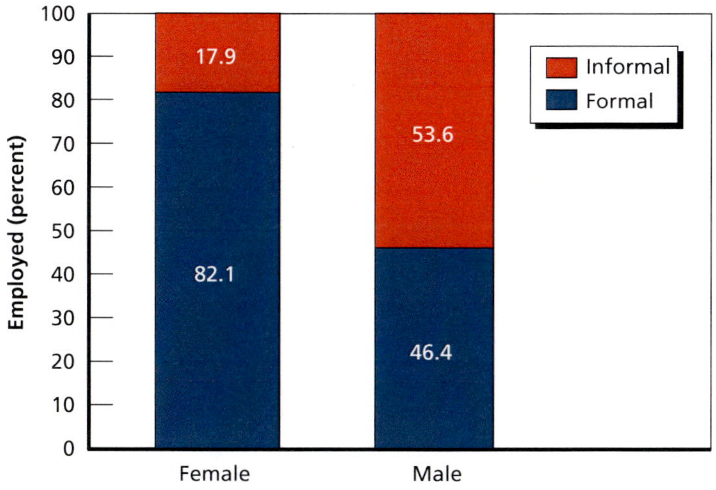

SOURCE: KRLFS.
RAND *RR293-5.10*

Employment by Ownership Sector

As in most economies of the region, public-sector employment is a dominant source of employment in the KRI: Approximately one-half of the working population (50.5 percent) is found in the public sector (Figure 5.11).[8] Since, as noted earlier, almost all formal jobs are public-sector jobs, this figure closely tracks the share of formal employment in the economy.[9] Note that this includes the significant military sector; without this category, the public sector accounts for 37 percent of all employment. Private-sector employment accounts for almost all nongovernment jobs in the economy, with no more than 1 percent in other sectors (e.g., nongovernmental organizations). Employment in foreign-owned firms accounts for just a tiny share—less than 1 percent—of employment in the KRI.

Within the public sector, employment in the military plays a prominent role, accounting for 26 percent of all public employment. Public (nonsecurity related) administration and support services account for 24 percent of public-sector jobs and education for 20 percent. Also noteworthy is that the vast majority of women who are working—82 percent—are found in the public sector, compared to only 45 percent of men. This accords with the greater presence of men in the informal sector, which is largely private.

Reflecting the presence of the capital city Erbil, Erbil governorate has the highest prevalence of public-sector jobs, amounting to 55.4 percent of all employment. The share of public-

[8] The following sectors are categorized as "government" for the sectoral calculations: government, state-owned enterprise, mixed private-public (e.g., public agency working for a private company, or publicly owned but privately managed), and military.

[9] The shares of formal jobs and public jobs are, in fact, both about 50 percent. This may seem inconsistent with the fact that not all (about 90 percent) formal jobs are public. If all public jobs are in the formal sector but there are also formal jobs that are not public, the number (and share) of formal jobs would have to exceed that of public jobs. However, a small portion of public-sector jobs are not formal by our definition, that is, the respondent indicates that no benefits are received or contract given. Alternative, firm-based definitions would yield a slightly different picture.

Figure 5.11
Employment by Ownership Sector

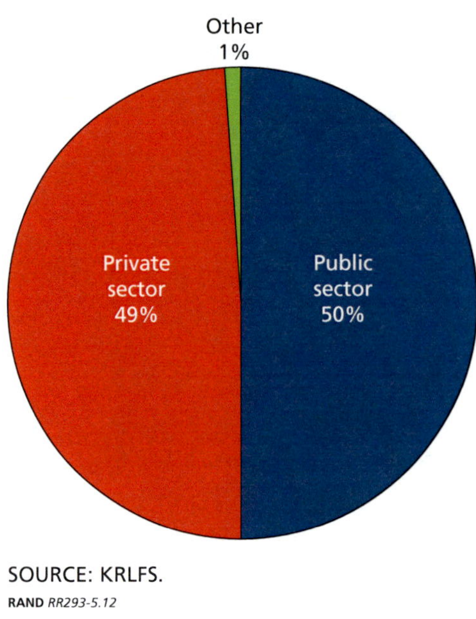

SOURCE: KRLFS.
RAND *RR293-5.12*

sector jobs in total employment is lowest in Sulaymaniya (about 46 percent), and the share in Duhok is 52.0 percent.

Employment by Activity Sector

We turn now to analysis by industrial or economic activity sector. By far, most employment in the KRI—almost three-fourths of all employment—is found in the services sector, as Figure 5.12 shows. Industry is a distant second (17.95 percent), followed by agriculture (6.63 percent).

The most important source of service-sector employment in the KRI is the military, accounting for 18 percent of all service employment and 13 percent of employment overall in the KRI. This is followed by public administration and support services (17 percent of all service employment) and education (13 percent). Within the smaller industrial sector, construction dominates, accounting for three-fourths (74 percent) of industrial employment. Manufacturing accounts for 8.7 percent of industrial employment and less than 2 percent of all employment in the KRI.

The overall shares of services, industry, and agriculture are consistent across governorates, with modest variations (Table 5.4). Agriculture accounts for a higher proportion of employment in Sulaymaniya (7.7 percent) than the other two governorates and has the smallest share in Erbil (4.9 percent). Perhaps more noteworthy than this variation, however, is the generally low share of agriculture in all governorates. The proportion of workers in service jobs is highest in Erbil (78.9 percent), reflecting in part that it includes the capital and hence has a relatively high share of public-sector jobs. On the other hand, Erbil has the lowest share of industrial employment (16.1 percent), compared to 19.4 percent in Duhok and 18.8 percent in Sulaymaniya.

With regard to patterns by gender (Figure 5.13), while most workers of either gender are found in services, the proportion for women is higher: 88 percent compared to 73.0 percent for

Figure 5.12
Percentage of Employment by Sector of Activity

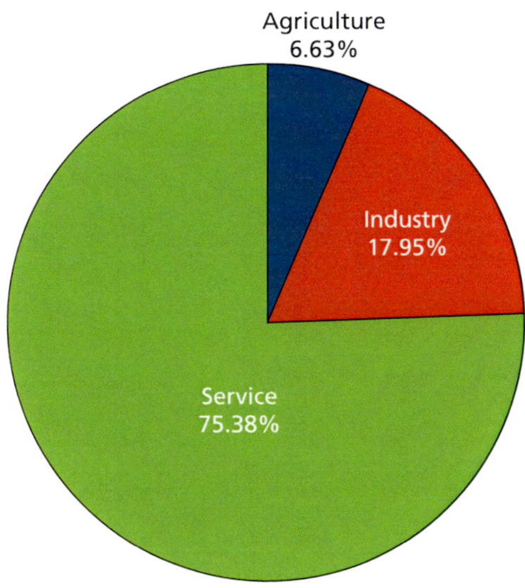

SOURCE: KRLFS.
RAND RR293-5.12

Table 5.4
Employment by Sector of Economic Activity, by Governorate (percent)

Sector	All KRI	Duhok	Sulaymaniya	Erbil
Agriculture	6.63	7.1	7.7	4.9
Industry	17.95	19.4	18.8	16.1
Services	75.38	73.5	73.4	78.9

SOURCE: KRLFS.

males. This reflects the patterns seen above, in which women in the workforce are more likely than men to be in public (hence service-sector) employment. In contrast, the smaller industrial sector is composed almost completely of men: Approximately 20.4 percent of male employment occurs in industrial activities, compared to only 3.3 percent for female employment. The share of employment in agriculture is low for both (6.3 percent of male employment versus 8.8 percent for women). Again, the findings point to very large differences in how men and women are situated in the labor market in Kurdistan.

Workshops and Capacity Building

In late July 2012, shortly after data collection and prior to analysis, RAND led two workshops for the KRSO focusing on (1) labor market concepts and indicators and (2) statistical analysis

Figure 5.13
Employment by Sector of Economic Activity, by Gender (percent shares)

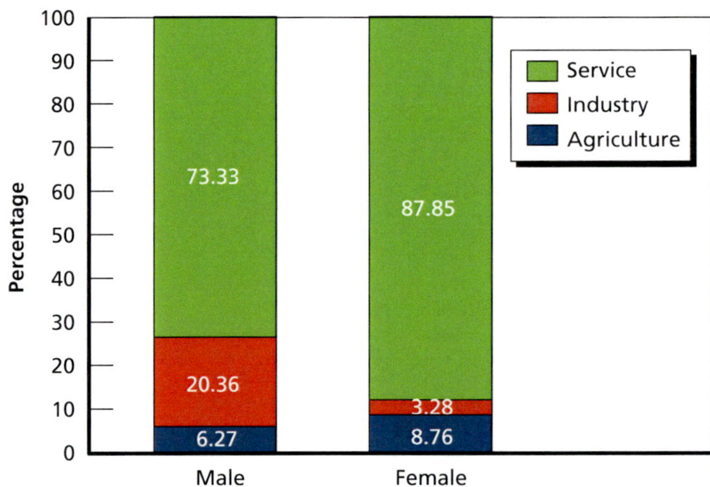

SOURCE: KRLFS.
RAND *RR293-5.13*

of labor force data.[10] The goal of the workshops was to enable the KRSO staff to conduct independent analysis of labor force surveys. The first workshop covered

- the meaning of the fundamental concepts in labor force analysis
- formalizing definitions of these concepts
- applying concept definitions to survey items; this involved using and combining survey questions to indicate whether a respondent fell into a given category (i.e. whether an individual should be considered unemployed)
- choosing which results to present
- how to present results.

The second workshop focused on statistical analysis of survey data. It covered the following subtopics:

- the implications of complex surveys: weighting and variances
  - For this topic, the implications of stratifying in survey design for analysis were reviewed, as well as the use of weights to calculate the correct means and variances and examples of how to do so.
- statistical analysis methods
  - This part of the workshop included how to create confidence intervals, significance tests, and correlations. There was an extensive discussion on how to use these methods to assess the reliability of results and how to report confidence intervals.

The KRSO staff from the central offices attended the workshops, which we directed at analysts who were going to work with the KRLFS data. To ensure that these individuals got

[10] Appendixes I and J, respectively, provide materials from these workshops.

hands-on experience in constructing labor force indicators and reporting results, it was agreed that, following the training and intensive discussions, the RAND and KRSO teams would conduct separate analyses of the data, compare results, and make refinements as needed. This process has continued, with frequent communication between the teams. Analysis is perhaps the most difficult area in which to build capacity because it depends heavily on existing levels of training and skills (particularly in statistics). However, through the efforts of the dedicated KRSO staff, considerable progress has been made. Over time, we have found increasing concordance between the results and the analysis the RAND and KRSO teams conducted independently.

A Template for Reporting Results

Also as part of the analysis phase of the study, RAND worked with the KRSO on a template for regularly reporting key employment indicators to the public and within the KRG. This is common practice among national statistics agencies. The presentation of findings should be clear and nontechnical to be accessible to a wide audience, and the overall presentation should be brief and concise.[11] It is possible to add or alter a select number of items, as desired, around the core statistics shown.

Summary

This chapter presented some of the main results from the first round of the KRLFS, including regional unemployment statistics and subgroup analysis. The RAND team conducted the analysis here, but KRSO staff conducted a parallel analysis. The joint analysis process served to build capacity through "learning by doing" that will enable the KRSO to analyze future rounds of the KRLFS and report the results within the KRG and to the public in the KRI. The data from the KRLFS can be used for more detailed analysis than that presented here, including tracking labor force characteristics over time as future rounds are collected; more-detailed analyses of population subgroups, sector, and industry; and analysis of earnings. All these will enhance informed policymaking.

The key results from the first survey can be summarized as follows:

- Participation in the labor force is relatively low in the KRI—just 38 percent of adults aged 15 and older. This is driven in large part by very low female participation (12 percent).
- The unemployment rate is 7.4 percent. While not low, this rate compares favorably with most countries in the Middle East.
- Among youth aged 15–24, however, unemployment is much higher (17.6 percent) than for adults 25 and older.
- The public sector dominates the KRI economy, accounting for about 50 percent of all employment and almost all (91 percent) private formal work. The private formal sector thus remains significantly underdeveloped.

---

[11] See Appendix D for the template.

- Industrial employment accounts for a modest (19 percent) share of employment, which instead is dominated by services (including government employment), which accounts for almost 75 percent of all employment.
- Women are situated very differently from men in the labor market. They participate in the labor force at a much lower rate and have a higher rate of unemployment; when women work, they are much more likely to work in the public sector than men are. Opportunities in the labor market, especially in private employment, may be quite limited for women, although their own or family preferences may also play a role in these patterns.

CHAPTER SIX

Recommendations for an Enterprise Survey

Objective

The KRSO is planning to conduct a survey of small and large establishments, in coordination with the CSO in Baghdad, based on questionnaires the CSO has developed for this purpose.[1] In RAND's previous project to support data collection for policymaking in the KRI, we stressed the importance of having a reliable measure of GDP as an indicator for monitoring the performance of the KRI economy. We therefore propose modifying the survey so that, in addition to gathering valuable information on enterprises, it can contribute to the calculation of GDP for the KRI.

A Cross-Country Comparison of Enterprise Surveys for GDP Calculation

With some modifications, the existing KRSO/CSO establishment survey questionnaire could be used to calculate GDP using the production approach. This approach estimates GDP by aggregating the value firms add to the economy; *value added* is the value of output net of costs of materials and services used in production (i.e., net of the costs of intermediate goods). The production approach is the most common method used for calculating regional GDP and the one most European Union countries use. One of its main advantages for regional GDP calculation is that it eliminates the need for data on interregional flows, which are typically difficult to obtain.

The other two main approaches for calculating GDP are the income approach, which estimates the incomes of individuals residing in the region, and the expenditure approach, which estimates the sum of all the expenditures households, firms, and government make in the region. In principle, all three methods will yield the same estimate of regional GDP. However, the expenditure approach requires data on interregional flows, while the income approach requires accurate information on household and firm incomes, which are also difficult to gather. For these reasons, the production approach is the most appropriate method for calculating regional GDP in the KRI.

While we examined establishment surveys from many countries, we confine our detailed comparisons here to two representative cases: Bahrain, in the Middle East, and New Zealand,

[1] We use the terms *enterprises*, *firms*, and *establishments* interchangeably. In reality, each enterprise or firm could have multiple establishments. The information that we would gather from the headquarters of the enterprise or the firm could be different from what we would gather from one of its subsidiary establishments.

which is at the global forefront of regional GDP calculation using establishment surveys.[2] A comparison of the current KRSO/CSO establishment survey questionnaire to those from these two countries, shown in Table 6.1, sheds light on some of the limitations of the survey for the purposes of GDP calculation. The current survey is similar to the one Bahrain uses, which is geared toward estimating manufacturing production, but it differs considerably from the one New Zealand uses.

For GDP calculation, the existing KRSO/CSO establishment survey may be more complicated than necessary. It asks for substantial amounts of information that is not needed for that purpose, such as full descriptions of quantities and values of production, sales and inventory, and number of employees. It therefore places an unnecessary reporting burden on the businesses, instead of asking only for the main values of interest: total income, expenses, and change in capital (which is related to investment). Such a burden could potentially lower the survey response rate. On the other hand, focusing the survey only on the basic parameters needed to estimate the GRP would mean not gathering other important information from the surveyed firms, especially on employment and a range of constraints facing firms. If integrated with other labor market information, such data can provide useful employer-employee information. Clearly, both needs would have to be balanced. For purposes of national and regional accounting and for a better understanding of the financial health of firms, it would have been more beneficial to ask about other financial issues, such as dividend payments, cash balance, and debt position.

Recommendations

For the purposes of efficiently estimating regional GDP, a top priority for the KRG, we recommend modifying the current establishment survey questionnaire as follows:

1. **Content adjustment.** The questionnaire should focus on three categories describing the economic position and activity of the establishment—income, expenditures, and capital stock—similar to the New Zealand Annual Enterprise Survey. For GDP purposes, the survey can eliminate the request for a full description of quantities and values of production, sales and inventory, and data on employees. Resources permitting, additional data on assets, liabilities, and equity should be collected.
2. **Sector-specific surveys.** Since business activity varies among various sectors (for example, agriculture, manufacturing, and services), the KRSO should tailor the survey for roughly five major sectors, starting with a core questionnaire, which could then be adapted to each sector. Special thought should be put toward developing a specific survey for the service sector, which is fairly different from manufacturing.
3. **Sampling design**. The sampling would have to be designed carefully, including stratifying by the major sectors (services, agriculture, trade and transport, mining and manufacturing, and construction). We recommend surveying all large firms (there are rela-

[2] Data sources were Kingdom of Bahrain Central Informatics Organization, "The Bahrain Industrial Production Survey for Manufacturing Establishments," website, 2007, and Statistics New Zealand, "New Zealand Annual Enterprise Survey 2010/2011," website, 2011.

Table 6.1
Comparison of KRSO/CSO, Bahrain, and New Zealand Establishment Surveys

Country	Iraq/KRI	Bahrain	New Zealand
Name of survey	The Small Industrial Establishment Form Economic and Financial Form/All Sectors (Medium and Large Establishments)	Industrial Production Survey for Manufacturing Establishments 2007	Annual Enterprise Survey 2010/11
Purpose	Multiple	Mainly, manufacturing index	National accounts
Types of establishments	All sizes, geared toward manufacturing	All sizes, geared toward manufacturing	Separate surveys for each type of activity (e.g., services, nonprofits, retails, manufacturing)
Level of detail	High regarding production: asks to specify each product and input used, and if product is finished or not	Relatively High: asks to specify each product and input used	Medium: Interested in aggregate income/expenditure. Asks for a breakdown by predefined categories
Number of workers asked?	Yes, plus breakdowns	Yes, plus breakdowns	No
Main chapters and tables	1. Fixed assets 1. Projects in progress 1. Change in inventory 1. Quantities and values of products, sales, and commodity inventory 1. Unfinished products, by-products 1. Quantities and values of other needs (various categories) 1. Service needs 1. Commodities produced 1. Raw materials provided by other parties 1. Revenues from service activities 1. Transferred revenues and other revenues 1. Commercial activity expenses and revenues 1. Transferred expenses 1. Interests and land rents 1. Subsidies and indirect taxes 1. Number of workers and their wages during the year 1. Benefits paid to workers during the year	1. Value and quantity of the production 1. Other services provided for others 1. Unit price—quantity of production—value of the major product or item 1. Raw materials 1. Consumption of goods and services 1. Taxes & fees and subsidiaries 1. Number of employees 1. Compensation of employees 1. Fixed assets and depreciation 1. Inventories	1. Income 1. Expenditure 1. Opening and closing stocks (=capital) 1. Surplus or deficit calculation 1. Dividends 1. Fixed assets 1. Intangible assets 1. Capital work undertaken by own employees 1. Assets (financial statement) 1. Equity and liabilities (financial statement)
Financial statements: cash, debt, dividends	No	No	Yes
Unique concepts (compared to others)			Intangible Assets Capital work undertaken by own employees Also: royalties, patent licenses

tively few) and taking a random sample of small and medium enterprises, as is currently planned for the KRSO/CSO survey.

4. **Complementary administrative data.** As is common in international best practice, GDP calculation in the KRI could be improved if the KRSO complements the survey data collection with administrative data (for example, using government budget data for government activities). Indeed, there would be a need to do so.
5. **Special treatment of interregional enterprises.** Consideration needs to be given to enterprises that operate across Iraqi regions and across international borders. For some of these cases, especially where surveying is difficult, the KRSO would need to adopt a "top-down" approach, which involves starting with Iraq-wide data and allocating the appropriate portions of the enterprises' activity to the KRI.

Summary

While the current KRSO/CSO establishment survey questionnaire would gather much useful information, we recommend streamlining the survey and modifying it to be more useful for calculating the KRI's GDP. We also recommend creating a core questionnaire, which can then be adapted to the major sectors of the economy.

CHAPTER SEVEN

Conclusions and Next Steps

This report has documented RAND's activities to improve data collection and reporting in the KRI. The overarching goal of this work was to assist the KRSO in developing capacity while producing valuable data for policymaking. We worked closely with the KRSO and in consultation with relevant ministries to prepare, conduct, and analyze a survey critical to policymaking by the KRG, the KRLFS, from start to finish. This survey will enable ongoing monitoring of trends in labor force participation, unemployment, and other indicators for the region.

Our work with the KRSO focused on complementing its existing strong expertise in survey field implementation, developed over multiple large-scale surveys in recent years, with enhanced capabilities in the areas of sampling, questionnaire development, data analysis, and reporting. By being involved in the complete "life cycle" of the survey, from conception through data collection to policy analysis, and by being responsible for the final execution and analysis of the surveys, the KRSO staff learned by doing.

The report covered the design of the sampling approach for the KRLFS; (2) the development of the survey questionnaire; (3) data collection, cleaning, and validation; (4) analysis of the KRLFS data to assess key labor force indicators; and (5) development of recommendations for a KRI establishment survey. As described in the report, activities (1) through (4) were carried out in close collaboration with the KRSO. This interaction took place through a series of five intensive workshops held at the KRSO headquarters and through frequent communications over the life of the project.

The KRSO carried out the first round of the KRLFS successfully in July 2012, with a second round in December 2012. Analysis of the data from the first round highlighted a number of important characteristics of the KRI labor force and economy, including low overall participation in the labor force, especially of women; an overall unemployment rate (7.4 percent) that is low relative to those of most countries in the Middle East; significantly higher unemployment among youth and among women; the dominance of the public sector as a source of employment and the contrasting small role of the private formal sector; and the predominant role of service-sector employment, which accounts for three-fourths of all work.

Our interactions with the KRSO staff throughout the first and second surveys lead us to conclude that considerable capacity had been built. This is indicated by the complexity of the issues staff members raised in discussions with us as the project proceeded and by the tasks they successfully completed on their own. The subsequent rounds of the KRLFS surveys that the KRSO staff have conducted independently are perhaps the most convincing evidence of such capacity building. The KRSO has made adjustments to the questionnaire, done the necessary sampling work (including choosing new RGs), cleaned the data, and carried out analysis along the same lines as for the first survey. Still, as expected, some areas are less developed than others. The main areas where further capacity could be built are data analysis and dissemination. At present, the KRSO staff are capable of generating and reporting on a wide range of labor statistics, including all those discussed earlier. We would like to see the KRSO gain additional skills for analyzing key topics, such as the determinants of earnings and participation and modeling of trends in various indicators, in more depth.

Future rounds of the KRLFS will provide up-to-date information on how important labor market indicators are changing over time and in response to policies. At the same time, continued implementation of the survey will help enhance the KRSO's capabilities in data collection, analysis, and reporting and serve as the basis for other survey collection efforts to meet specific needs for information.

Looking ahead, we recommend the following steps to build on the successful implementation of the KRLFS and other areas of progress made so far:

- Implement subsequent rounds of the KRLFS, adhering to a regular, quarterly schedule, and systematize methods for rapid analysis and reporting of results to policymakers and the public.
- Deepen the KRSO analytical capabilities, through future workshops and other means, to cover other topics that will enhance both analysis and reporting, such as correlation and regression analysis and integration of spatial mapping (graphical information systems) with survey data (to better understand differences across areas in economic activity and needs).
- In general, it is important to maintain and upgrade any capacity built. Workshops, training sessions, higher degree programs in foreign universities in some cases, and continuing learning by doing are ways to achieve this goal. (Along these lines, the KRG has been funding three senior analysts from the KRSO to study in England for master's degrees in statistics.)
- Consider investigating several other topics of policy interest using the first and subsequent rounds of data, including the determinants of wages and earnings in different sectors of the labor market and for different groups (for example, public- versus private-sector pay) and the factors associated with the participation of men, women, and youth in the labor force and in different sectors of the economy. These topics can be addressed using basic descriptive statistical analysis but are best addressed with multivariate regression approaches that allow controls for differences among individuals. Participating in this analysis will deepen the KRSO's analytical capabilities, as noted earlier.
- Work with the KRSO to be able to flexibly identify and address other critical areas via appropriate data collection and analysis. The objective is to make the KRSO a responsive organization that can respond to changing needs for data and analysis on its own, without relying on direction from multilateral organizations.
- A key area that has been identified, as discussed in this report, is the need for reliable GDP calculations for the KRI using enterprise surveys. The KRSO will lead the survey effort, and should also develop the capacity for generating GDP and other key statistics from these surveys.

The longitudinal data that are being collected on the KRI labor force will have a wealth of information on patterns and trends in the labor market, which can be analyzed in more detail than we did for this summary report. As mentioned earlier, the scope of the study was limited to identifying basic patterns in the labor market, rather than exploring specific issues in detail or the factors underlying the observed patterns. Analyzing the data with a view toward identifying the forces behind the labor market situation observed in the KRSO would be a fruitful research avenue for both the KRSO and RAND.

APPENDIX A

Sampling Design

Objective

To select a probability sampling approach that will produce estimates of the unemployment rate, labor force participation rate, and related variables for population and subpopulations of interest in the KRI with reasonable precision (or ME).

Strata of Interest and Stratification

A *stratum* is a subgroup of homogeneous (similar) units within the larger population for which key statistics are to be calculated. The strata can be defined geographically (e.g., governorate or district) or along other lines, such as gender and age. The total sample size needed for the survey will depend on the key strata for which statistics are desired. For this discussion, the specific strata of interest, for which we desire estimates with acceptable precision, are as follows:

- governorate
- district
- age groups (15–30, 31–49, 50–64)
- gender
- urban or rural.

We will also estimate these statistics for the intersection of a few strata:

- gender with urban or rural (e.g., women in rural areas)
- age groups with urban or rural (e.g., ages 15–30 in urban areas)
- governorate with urban or rural (e.g., rural population in Duhok).

Explicit stratification in sampling divides the population into strata—for example, by district or by rural or urban location of residence. Separate samples are then randomly selected from each stratum. This is in contrast to simple random sampling (SRS), which draws the random sample from the population as a whole. Stratification improves the precision of the survey estimates. It also guarantees representation of the individual subpopulations or strata because the numbers from each are determined beforehand, rather than being left to chance as they would be with SRS.

We conducted the sampling with explicit stratification on the district, following most previous household surveys conducted in the region. Therefore, the population was divided by district (KRI has 33), with separate random samples from each district.

For other subgroups of interest, such as age, gender, and rural or urban location, the sample was not explicitly stratified. The sample sizes for these strata were determined by their prevalence in the population or their "marginal distributions." One reason for not stratifying here, other than the technical difficulties of stratifying on multiple categories, is that these broad subgroups generally will be adequately represented once the explicit stratification by districts is done.

It is desirable to ensure adequate precision (acceptable ME) for measured outcomes in each of the strata of interest. However, the cost of ensuring the *same* level of high precision in each stratum might be too high, meaning the required sample size would be very large. We therefore had to exercise appropriate judgment in determining acceptable precision for different strata (and different outcomes). Policy considerations should drive such decisions—for what subpopulations do policymakers most need accurate information?

Multistage Survey Design and Clustering

Once we determined how many households were to be randomly sampled in each stratum (district, in our case), how were these households selected? The approach used in household-based surveys in the KRI and elsewhere is the multistage cluster design. This approach begins with random selection of primary sampling units (PSUs) from a listing of all PSUs. In the KRI, as in most other contexts, PSUs are enumeration areas from the national population census. PSUs are also known as *survey clusters*. Once the PSUs are selected, a sample of households is randomly selected within each PSU. The households are known as secondary sampling units (SSUs).

One reason for the two-stage design is to reduce the cost of fieldwork; it is much cheaper to interview groups of households that are located near each other (in the same cluster) than to randomly select and interview households from the overall population. A second reason, also cost related, is that, because the census may be out of date, it is typically necessary to update the list of households for the survey before drawing the sample. With the two-stage design and clustering, it is only necessary to update the listings for clusters selected for the survey, rather than all the clusters or enumeration areas in the census.

In the KRI, the PSUs are census enumeration areas, or *blocks*. The Census Frame from 2011 provides a list of these blocks and counts of household members within each block. The survey updated these lists for the selected PSUs and select households within them by SRS.

Proportionate Versus Disproportionate Stratification

The 33 districts of the KRI have substantially varying populations. For example, the two largest districts, Hawler Center in Erbil and Sulaymaniya Center in Sulaymaniya, each have about 100 times the population of the two smallest districts. The proportionate-to-size sampling approach allocates to each district the same share of the sample as its share of the overall population. That is, it applies a common sampling rate (or percentage of households) to all districts.

Therefore, sampling weights are not needed to calculate statistics at various levels. However, the great variation in district sizes means that some districts would contribute very few, and others too many, households to the overall sample. Constraining the total sample size to a range between 5,000 and 7,000 households means that smaller districts would end up with insufficient sample sizes to give reasonable MEs in district-level estimates of labor force participation and unemployment rates.

Therefore, we opted for a disproportionate allocation strategy, which samples at a higher rate in smaller districts, causing them to be overrepresented in the sample (and correspondingly, larger districts to be somewhat underrepresented). The advantage of disproportionate as opposed to proportionate sampling is that it ensures a specified or minimum district-level precision. The disadvantage is that weighting is needed to produce national or other higher-level (e.g., governorate) estimates so that each district represents its correct share of the population. The effects of weighting are to increase the standard error and to reduce the precision of the national or other higher-level estimates, through the design effect (DEFF) (discussed later). The more we diverge from proportional allocation, the less precise are the national or higher-level estimates. An additional challenge of the disproportionate scheme is that it requires careful thought about how to distribute the total sample across districts or sample allocation, based on detailed empirical calculations.

A common and simple form of disproportionate sampling across strata, used in the 2007 and 2012 IHSES, is *equal allocation*, in which the same number of households is drawn from each district (about 200 in the case of the IHSES). This approach involves selecting a single sample size for all districts to ensure an equal, acceptable level of precision in the district-level estimates. To explore this, we calculated a minimum sample size for a district under a disproportionate sampling scheme with equal allocation. Given the required size per district, multiplying this by the number of districts (33) produces the required total sample size. We estimated that a total sample size of 6,600 households (i.e., 200 households × 33 districts) would ensure a level of precision or margin of error of 5 percent in each district.

However, given the disparities in district populations noted above, this approach would lead to sampling the smallest districts at fully 100 times the rate of the largest districts. Due to the very high rates of over- and undersampling and the resulting high variance in sampling weights that follow, the calculations indicated a significant loss of precision in the national estimates. Further, while the smaller districts would be large enough to obtain reasonable MEs by design, we wished to do better for large districts (have larger samples and hence more precision, especially for subgroups), since by virtue of their size these areas are economically more important. Therefore we used this estimate of 6,600 households as a starting point for the final estimates, making adjustments as described next.

To avoid the problems associated with the extremes of proportionate sampling on the one hand and equal allocation on the other, many survey designs adopt a compromise between these two schemes. One compromise would be to use a proportionate strategy overall but raise the sample sizes for the smaller strata to obtain some minimum level. Another would be to specify a maximum sample size for districts, reducing the sample size for the largest districts.

Kish, 1988, advocates a more-flexible variant of this idea for strata of highly varying sizes. The allocation to district h would then be proportional to

$$n\sqrt{W_h^2 + \frac{1}{H^2}},$$

where n is the total sample size; W_h is the proportion of the total population in district h; and H is the total number of districts (33 in the KRI). This formula allocates more of the sample to more-populous districts while moderating this effect as the number of districts increases. As described further below, we used this approach, setting the total sample n to 7,000 households. We made one additional modification, setting a maximum sample size of 400 for the largest districts so as to allocate the sample more equally. This reduces the number of households only for the two largest districts, and the households "removed" from these districts are then distributed evenly over the rest of the districts. Under this allocation, the smallest districts have 160 households, and the largest, as noted, have 400. While we describe the sample size calculations in detail below, we summarize the conclusions here:

- An *equal allocation* scheme, assuming enrollment of the minimum number of households per district to achieve a 5-percent ME for labor force participation and 4.4 percent for unemployment, requires a total sample size of 6,600 households. The DEFF of weighting under this approach is a high 2.50. The DEFF implies that the variance of estimates under this scheme is 2.5 times the variance obtained under a proportionate sampling scheme, without weights.
- The scheme using the modified Kish approach for 7,000 households and setting a maximum for the larger districts of 400 households has a smaller DEFF, 1.58, from weighting (ensuring very precise subgroup as well as national-level estimates) and still allows a moderate level of precision for smaller districts. The reduction in variance can be directly estimated from the reduction in DEFF from 2.5 to 1.58.

We recommended the second approach, primarily because of better precision within subgroups (for example, unemployment rate in rural areas of Duhok). It is also more efficient for national estimates than the first approach. For district-level estimates, it guarantees high precision (ME of 3.5 percent) for the largest districts and tolerable precision (7.5-percent ME) for the smallest districts. The overall sample size of 7,000 is still reasonable from the viewpoint of survey costs and demands on human and other resources of KRSO.

In contrast, all previous household surveys done in the KRI of which we are aware seem to have followed equal allocation across districts. However, as noted, the disadvantages of equal allocation are a loss of efficiency for subgroup and national or other higher-level estimates as a result of forcing the same sample size and level of precision for the largest districts as for the smallest. The second approach is therefore a reasonable compromise between completely proportionate and completely equal allocation designs.

Parameters Used in Sample-Size Calculations

While calculating estimates of required sample sizes, it is best to use as much information as is available from previous surveys or other data sources. However, if this is not possible, it is necessary to assume reasonable values for the necessary inputs based on data from other countries or educated guesses. This, in turn, requires a sensitivity analysis, varying the values to see how the required sample size changes. The essential parameters needed for the sample-size calculations are

1. means and variances of the outcomes of interest (here, labor force participation and unemployment rates)
2. ICC
3. average number of individuals per household and composition by gender and age.

Fortunately, for the KRI, previous surveys—the IHSES 2007 and the 2008 employment survey—are available, so we were able to get the above information from actual data. The data used in the calculations are given in a separate Excel sheet.

We also set two other parameters for the calculations:

1. acceptable level of precision, or ME
2. number of households or sample size per cluster.

The following subsections discuss all these parameters in detail.

Mean and Variances of Outcomes

We derived the following from IHSES, 2007:

1. estimated labor force participation rate in the KRI (mean 42.39 percent, variance 0.49)
2. estimated unemployment rate among those in the labor force in the KRI (mean 11.9 percent, variance 0.32).

The means indicated here are for the adult population (men and women aged 15 and over) for the KRI as a whole. Our calculations below also use means from the IHSES for different subgroups of interest, such as men and women and individuals in different age groups.

Intracluster Correlation

The fact that households within a cluster tend to be similar in terms of the outcomes of interest tends to reduce the overall variation in the sample relative to the case of no clustering, as in an SRS. This decreases the efficiency or precision of the estimates. We expect households or individuals within a cluster to resemble one another because two people living in the same area will tend to face similar opportunities or constraints and behave more similarly than two people from different locations. In statistical terms, the ICC measures the correlations of outcomes among units within a cluster. It is best thought of in terms of analysis of variance. If individuals are organized into groups (i.e., survey clusters) and if we divide the total variance in the outcome into variation that is "within groups" and "between groups," the ICC is the proportion of the total variance that is "between groups." When the ICC is high, most of the variation comes from differences between groups, rather than from differences among individuals within groups (a high ICC means individuals are more similar within groups).

The ICC is relevant to our sample size calculations because, as discussed under "Multistage Survey Design and Clustering," the two-stage survey design organizes the sample into clusters based on census enumeration areas. If individuals within clusters are very similar, there will not be much variation, thereby substantially decreasing the precision relative to SRS when there is no clustering. This, in turn, requires a larger sample—sometimes substantially larger—to obtain estimates with a given ME. This is discussed further under "Description of Sample-Size Calculations," which shows how the ICC is incorporated into the sample size calculations to account for the effects of clustering.

The ICC also has implications for choosing the number of households per cluster. If the ICC is high, increasing the sample size by adding more households to each cluster will not add much to the overall variation in the outcome, hence will not greatly improve precision of estimates. It would be much more effective (since it would increase variation more) to increase sample size by adding more clusters to the sample.

Note that the ICC can potentially differ for the labor force participation and unemployment rates. The ICC estimates for indicators of labor force participation and unemployment were estimated with the IHSES, 2007, data using hierarchical logistic models with Xcluster command in STATA (using the cluster indicator in IHSES, 2007, as the clustering variable). These models allow us to see how much within-group versus between-group differences explain labor force participation and unemployment outcomes. We estimated the ICC to be 0.0268 and 0.0335 for labor force participation and unemployment, respectively, and used these values for the sample size calculations.

Average Number of Individuals per Household

Ultimately, the sample for the analysis is a collection of individuals, not households. For example, we are interested in labor force participation among adult men and women, or among youth aged 15–19. However, the sampling is done in terms of households (which are the SSUs), which requires determining how many households it takes to get the necessary number of individuals. To illustrate with a simple example, if we need 10,000 adults age 15 and over to calculate the labor force participation rate with a desired ME and if there are an average of 2.5 adults per household, we would need to sample 4,500 households (10,000 ÷ 2.5). Similar calculations would be done for subgroups of interest, e.g., youth or women versus men, using the average number of persons of each type per household of that type.

Here, too, we were able to rely on a previous survey for information on average number of individuals per household and composition. We used demographic information from IHSES, 2007. The average number of individuals per household aged 15 or older in Kurdistan in the IHSES is 3.77. Therefore, once we determined the desired sample size—the number of *individuals*—for estimating the overall adult labor force participation rate, we applied the conversion factor of (1 ÷ 3.77) to determine the number of households that needed to be in the survey. As described below, the unemployment rate, in contrast, is calculated only for those in the labor force. Therefore, the conversion factor will be 1 over the average number of labor force participants per household, which is 1.60 in the IHSES.

Similarly, we calculated average number of individuals in different age groups, number of men and women, and average number of other subgroups per households for the sample size calculations for those subgroups.

Margin of Error

ME is a confidence interval calculated for a statistic (such as the unemployment rate) that shows the range within which the true value will lie with a specified level of probability, typically 95 percent. The ME is one-half the width of the confidence interval. Both are used to express the amount of variability in an estimate of an outcome that is inherent in random sampling. As an illustration, assume we are told that the estimate of unemployment (the unemployment rate) is 15 percent with an ME of 3 percent. This means that there is a 95 percent probability that the *true* unemployment rate is in the interval of ±3 percent of the 15 percent estimate: That is, the true estimate is a value between 12 and 18 percent. The width of the confidence interval is 6 percent (18 percent to 12 percent), or twice the ME.

Since the variance of an estimate falls as sample size increases, a smaller ME requires a larger sample size. Sample size calculations proceed with determination of what the ME will be for different sample sizes or, alternatively, with specification of a desired ME for the outcome and calculating the sample size required to achieve that level of precision. We took the second approach and considered the sample size implications of four margins of error: 3 percent, 5 percent, 7.5 percent, and 10 percent. From an examination of ILO standards and other sources, we found the 3 percent rate to be a standard benchmark. While 3 percent seems like a demanding requirement, it is worth considering this from a policy perspective. As noted, for an unemployment rate of 15 percent, an ME of 3 percent means that we can be 95 percent certain that the true rate is between 12 percent and 18 percent. This is a fairly wide interval. If ME was allowed to be higher, at 5 percent, we could be reasonably certain only that the true rate is between 10 percent and 20 percent. Policymakers would no doubt consider there to be a very big difference between unemployment of 10 percent and 20 percent and would presumably like a more accurate estimate of the unemployment rate. Therefore, precision is important in the estimates. On the other hand, higher precision requires a bigger sample, and this can become costly or impractical. Therefore, we also calculated sample size requirements for MEs greater than 3 percent and up to 10 percent (as recommended by the United Nations for smaller surveys).

Sample Size per Cluster

As noted above, when households within a cluster are very similar (ICC is high), adding more households to each cluster does not do much to improve precision . It is more effective to keep the same number of households per cluster and add clusters. However, this has a cost in terms of fieldwork resources. Given the fixed costs of traveling to and working in a cluster, it is easier to add households to each cluster than to add clusters. For example, assume the sample had 1,000 households in 100 clusters of ten households each. Increasing sample size to 1,500 by adding 50 clusters would be more costly than simply interviewing five more households in each cluster. However, the first approach would vary the outcome more and, therefore, yield more precise estimates. Therefore, deciding between adding households to clusters or adding clusters involves a trade-off between cost and precision.

Previous surveys in the KRI have used around ten households per block (cluster), which is small relative to household surveys across the world (for which cluster size tends to range between ten and 25 households). Our sample size calculations considered two cluster sizes, ten and 15 households per block, amounting to about 38 and 57 individuals over 15 per cluster, respectively, for the overall labor force participation calculation. Applying the estimate of 1.75 persons per household in the workforce yields 16 and 24 persons per cluster for the unemployment rate calculations for the two cluster sizes.

Sample-Size Calculations

The tables at the end of this appendix carry out the sample size calculations described here. We consider the required sample size at the level of the district on which the sample will be stratified, as well as the implications for higher levels of aggregation, including for the entire KRI ("national" estimates). As we will show, aggregation involves the use of sample weights when combining multiple districts under disproportionate allocation, thus increasing the required sample size.

Total and District-Level Sample Sizes

We first need to calculate the sample we would need under SRS; this sample is also known as the effective sample size (ESS). For a binary variable, such as labor force participation or unemployment, the required sample size for an SRS is given by

$$ESS = \frac{z_{0.95}^{2} \times p(1-p)}{e^{2}}, \tag{1}$$

where p is the estimate of the mean of the outcome (here, the labor force participation rate or unemployment rate); e is the desired ME; and $Z_{0.95}$ is the z statistic for a 95-percent confidence interval, which is 1.96.

We next calculated the DEFF. As explained earlier, a two-stage clustered design needs a larger sample size than does the SRS to obtain a given level of precision; we then had to convert this sample size to what the clustered design actually needed. The conversion factor going from an SRS to a complex design is the DEFF associated with the design. The DEFF shows the proportional increase in the variance of the estimate relative to SRS.

By definition, the DEFF is the ratio of the variance of an estimate obtained via the complex (e.g., clustered) design over the variance of the same estimate obtained under an SRS. When the DEFF is greater than 1, the results are less precise than those with SRS. For a sample of m individuals from each cluster and an ICC of r, the DEFF due to clustering is

$$DEFF_c = 1 + (m-1) \times r. \tag{2}$$

The DEFF increases with r, as expected, because the correlation of observations within clusters leads to greater variance in the estimates. With no geographical clustering of observations (the SRS case), the ICC is zero and DEFF = 1. In this (unrealistic) case, there is no loss of precision relative to SRS.

It is important to note that, for a given total sample size, n, the DEFF also increases with m, the number of observations per cluster. Given the total sample size, more observations per cluster means fewer clusters overall in the sample. Since observations are similar within clusters, it is more desirable to have more clusters with fewer households per cluster than few clusters with many similar households per cluster.

National-level estimates require a second adjustment needed. This factor is a separate DEFF that arises from using (unequal) sample weights for different strata (districts). This DEFF, or $DEFF_W$, must be accounted for when we combine the district-level samples into one national sample. It is also needed for any other high-level estimate that combines districts, such as governorate-level estimates. It is calculated as follows:

$$DEFF_w = 1 + (CV_w)^2, \tag{3}$$

where CV_w is the coefficient of variation (or, standard deviation divided by the mean) of the district weights. Note that, as the weights become more unequal or variable (dispersed), this factor will also increase, holding the mean constant, and the larger sample size will be the required size to obtain a given level of precision. For equal sample sizes for all districts, weights would be highly unequal (the smallest districts need to be heavily downweighted and the largest heavily upweighted), and therefore $DEFF_W$ would be large.

Putting the two DEFFs together, the adjustment factor to convert a SRS sample size to the sample size under a complex design for the national-level estimates is

$$DEFF = DEFF_c \times DEFF_w. \tag{4}$$

To get the actual or nominal sample size required, n, multiply the ESS given by (1) with the combined DEFF given by (4):

$$n = ESS \times DEFF = \frac{z_{0.95}^2 \times p(1-p) \times DEFF}{e^2}. \tag{5}$$

Say that n is 1,000, and the DEFF is 1.5; this value of DEFF indicates that the variance of the estimate is inflated by 50 percent over SRS. The ESS is then 677; that is, the precision of the estimate is equivalent to what we would obtain with an SRS of only 677 observations.

To summarize, the steps involved incorporating the DEFFs to get the required sample size for national or other aggregate-level estimates are

1. Calculate the sample size that would be needed (given the desired ME) for the SRS sampling strategy. This is the ESS given by (1).
2. Calculate $DEFF_C$ to account for the clustered design, using (2).
3. Calculate $DEFF_w$ to account for the weighting or nonproportionate allocation across districts, using (3).
4. Multiply ESS by the total DEFF given by (4) to estimate n, the total sample size needed for national-level estimates.
5. Divide the sample size from step 4 (which is in terms of individuals) by the average number of individuals per household to get the required number of households.

Determining the required sample size for estimates to be reported at the district level uses the same procedure but leaves out step 3. Since this looks only at individual districts, $DEFF_w$ is not relevant. However, clustering still affects these district-level estimates, so $DEFF_C$ must be incorporated.

Sample Allocation Across Districts

The total sample has to be allocated across districts. The total sample size is calculated to ensure a high level of precision for national and other aggregated estimates (e.g., by governorate, by male versus female, by age group) and a reasonable level of precision for smaller districts. As noted in the "Proportionate Versus Disproportionate Stratification" subsection, there is a trade-off between these objectives, which led us to choose a modified Kish allocation rule.

We followed an iterative process to calculate this allocation. We started out with an objective of attaining a 5-percent ME for all district-level estimates under equal allocation of the sample across districts. This exercise resulted in an initial figure of 6,534 households for the total sample (Table A.1).

Recall that the Kish allocation rule calls for an allocation to districts proportional to

$$n\sqrt{W_h^2 + \frac{1}{H^2}}, \tag{6}$$

where n is the total sample size; W_h is the proportion of the total population in district h; and H is the total number of districts (33). We applied this rule to the total sample size of 6,534 households obtained above and then made two adjustments. One adjustment to the Kish allocation noted earlier was to set a maximum sample size of 400 for the largest districts so that they do not have too large an allocation. This reduces the number of households only for the two largest districts, and the households removed from these districts were then distributed evenly over the remaining districts. This adjustment makes the overall allocation slightly more equal than under the pure Kish rule.

Starting from the initial total sample above, we calculated MEs for various total sample sizes under our modified Kish allocation rule. A sample size of 7,000 was found to yield very precise estimates for national aggregates for labor force participation and unemployment, as well as generally very good MEs for regional (governorate) level estimates and estimates for population subgroups, such as youth and women. At the same time, this sample size permits reasonable precision at the district level for most districts, as described below. In our final proposal, therefore, we recommended a total sample size of 7,000 households with district sample sizes determined using the Kish rule, which resulted in a minimum district size of 160 households and a maximum of 400 (following the adjustment noted above). Table A.2 shows the resulting number of households and clusters (for ten households per cluster) in each of the 33 districts.

Tables A.3 and A.4 demonstrate the ME and associated effective sample size under a number of assumptions, for estimates at the district, national, and other levels.

Results of Calculations at the District Level

We will first discuss the district-level precision that our proposed allocation scheme implies. Sample size calculations for the labor force participation and unemployment rate will differ depending on the parameters mentioned earlier, under "Parameters Used in Sample-Size Calculations."

Labor Force Participation Rate

We used an estimate for p of 42.3 percent for the labor force participation rate calculations. Assuming ten households per cluster, the relevant m per cluster for equation (2) is 38 individuals (given an average of 3.77 adults aged 15 and older per household). For this value of m, $DEFF_C$ from equation (1) is 1.99. The necessary sample size for a district to have an ME of 5 percent, then, is 198 households. For purposes of fieldwork efficiency, increasing the number of households per cluster to 15 (yielding an m of 57) produces a substantially larger DEFF, 2.49, so a 5-percent ME would require a sample size of 247 households per district.

Under the modified Kish rule we adopted, the district-level sample sizes varied between 400 and 160 households. Thus, the associated ME varied between 3.5 percent and 5.6 percent for adult labor force participation.

Unemployment Rate

We used an estimate for *p* of 11.9 percent in the unemployment rate calculations. For a cluster of ten households, 16 persons will be in the labor force per cluster (average of 1.60 per household), and the DEFF from clustering will be 1.50. Under these assumptions, achieving an n ME of 5 percent requires a sample size of 149 households. Increasing the number of households units per cluster to 15 yields a DEFF of 1.77, requiring a larger sample size, of 176 households, to achieve the same ME.

Under the modified Kish rule we adopted, the associated ME for district-level estimates varied between 3.1 and 5.0 percent for the unemployment rate.

Summary

Under an equal-allocation scheme, we estimated that we need a total sample size of 6,534 households to obtain an ME of 5 percent and 4.4 percent for labor force participation and unemployment, respectively. However, we also estimated that the associated "cost," or DEFF, of this sampling design is large ($DEFF_W = 2.5$) because the weights are highly unequal. $DEFF_W$ is significantly lower (1.58) for the modified Kish allocation. For the two largest districts, this scheme still ensures MEs of 3.5 percent and 3.1 percent for the labor force participation and unemployment rate estimates, respectively. For the two smallest districts, this will ensure MEs of 5.6 percent and 5.0 percent for the two estimates, respectively.

Results of Calculations for National-Level and Subgroup-Level Estimates Under the Modified Kish Design

Now we turn to the precision of the national- and governorate-level estimates under the proposed sampling scheme. Our final sample size estimate is 7,000 households, for a sample size of 26,390 individuals (7,000 × 3.77). Incorporating the two adjustment factors of $DEFF_C$ (1.99) and $DEFF_W$ (1.58) leads to an ESS of 8,393 individuals for the labor force participation rate estimates—(7,000 × 3.77) ÷ (1.99 × 1.58). The ESS for the unemployment rate is 3,562 individuals—(7,000 × 1.60) ÷ (1.99 × 1.58)—since the relevant number of individuals per household here is 1.60.

The ME for the overall national estimate of labor force participation is small, at 1.1 percent (first row of Table A.3). The 95-percent confidence interval around an estimated 42.3 percent labor force participation rate will be (41.3 percent, 43.4 percent). Similarly, the ME associated with the overall national estimate of unemployment rate is also small, at 1.1 percent (first row of Table A.4). The 95-percent confidence interval around an estimate of 11.9 percent will be 10.8 to 13.0 percent.

However, we wanted to evaluate whether this sampling scheme would produce adequate precision for the national and governorate statistics of interest, not just for the overall adult population but also by gender and age group. These subsamples, naturally, will yield less precise estimates than the total sample. In particular, we were concerned that strata that have a low representation in the population (e.g., persons aged 50–64 years and females in the labor force) may have small sample sizes and therefore inadequate precision. For the district-level calculations above, we assumed a certain precision and asked what the sample size needs to be.

Here, we took the total sample size as given and asked what the ME of the estimates will be for different subgroups.

We obtained estimates for labor force participation and unemployment rates (the p needed for our calculations) from the IHSES, 2007, data for the different subgroups (e.g., age, gender, urban/rural). Using the shares of these groups in the population and our total assumed sample of 7,000 households, we estimated the number of observations in each group/stratum in the sample. We assumed a 95-percent confidence level, as we did for Table A.1. Finally, we modified equation (1) slightly to compute the ME e for each subpopulation:

$$e = Z_{0.95} \times \sqrt{\frac{p \times (1-p)}{ESS}}. \qquad (7)$$

Results of Calculations for Subgroups

Labor Force Participation Rate

Table A.3 shows the results of these calculations for labor force participation. With the overall labor force participation rate estimated at 42.3 percent, the ME around this statistic is generally larger than for point estimates of unemployment rate because the binomial distribution has the largest variance at 50 percent. The ME did not exceed 5 percent for any of the estimates, which is a reasonable level of precision. Also, the ME exceeds the stricter threshold of 3 percent only for several strata: males aged 50–64, persons aged 50–64 in urban areas, persons 15–30 in a rural area, persons aged 31–49 in rural areas, persons aged 50–64 in rural areas, and estimates for rural areas for all three governorates. The table highlights cases where the ME exceeds 3 percent.

Unemployment Rate

Table A.4 shows the results of these calculations for unemployment. The overall unemployment rate is 11.9 percent. This statistic was calculated only for those in the labor force (42.3 percent of the total effective sample size). We found that the ME exceeded 5 percent for one stratum only: females aged 50–64. On the other hand, the ME exceeds 3 percent for females in all three age groups (15–30, 31–49, and 50–64), persons aged 50–64 in urban areas, persons in rural areas and aged 15–30 or 50–64, and estimates for rural areas for all three governorates. The larger margins of error for the rural, female, and ages 50–64 subgroups of the population are explained by the low prevalence of the groups in the population or their low rate of labor force participation, which reduces the sample. The table highlights an ME if it exceeds 3 percent. Overall, the proposed sampling scheme yields high levels of precision for most subgroups.

Table A.1
Effective Sample Calculations at the District Level

	ESS	Estimate (%)	SE	Z(95)	Margin of Error (%)	95 CI Lower Bound (%)	95 CI Upper Bound (%)	DEFFC-1	NSS-1	No. HH-1	DEFF-2	NSS-2	No. HH-2
National													
Est LFP	8,394	42.3	0.0054	1.96	1.06	41.3	43.4						
Est UE	3,552	11.9	0.0054	1.96	1.1	10.8	13.0						
District													
Estd. LFP	93	42.3	0.0512	1.96	10.0	32.3	52.4	1.99	185	49	2.49	231	61
	165	42.3	0.0385	1.96	7.5	34.8	49.9	1.99	328	87	2.49	410	109
	300	42.3	0.0285	1.96	5.6	36.7	47.9	1.99	597	158	2.49	746	198
	375	42.3	0.0255	1.96	5.0	37.3	47.3	1.99	747	198	2.49	933	247
	750	42.3	0.0180	1.96	3.5	38.8	45.9	1.99	1493	396	2.49	1,866	495
Estd. UE	39	11.9	0.0517	1.96	10.1	32.2	52.4	1.50	59	37	1.77	70	44
	70	11.9	0.0388	1.96	7.6	34.7	49.9	1.50	105	66	1.77	124	77
	127	11.9	0.0288	1.96	5.6	36.7	48.0	1.50	191	119	1.77	225	141
	159	11.9	0.0257	1.96	5.0	37.3	47.4	1.50	238	149	1.77	281	176
	317	11.9	0.0182	1.96	3.6	38.8	45.9	1.50	477	298	1.77	562	352
	425	11.9	0.0157	1.96	3.1	39.2	45.4	1.50	639	400	1.77	752	471

NOTES: Number of persons ages 15 and above in a household: 3.77.
Number of persons ages 15 and above in the labor force per household: 1.60.

Table A.1—Continued

Clustering in Indicator of Unemployment

ICC	Cluster Size	DEFF-Clustering
0.034	16	1.50
0.034	24	1.77

DEFF	ME (%)	HH/District	No. District	Min HH
1.55	3	423	33	13,959
1.55	5	149	33	4,917
1.85	3	499	33	16,467
1.85	5	177	33	5,841

Clustering in Indicator of Labor Force Participation

Est.ICC	Persons/cluster	DEFF-Clustering
0.027	38	1.99
0.027	57	2.49

DEFF	ME (%)	HH/District	No. District	Min HH
1.99	3	554	33	18,282
1.99	5	198	33	6,534
2.49	3	693	33	22,869
2.49	5	247	33	8,151

Table A.2
Number of Households by District Under the Modified Kish Allocation

	(1)	(2)	(3)	(4)	(5)	(6)	(7)	(8)
				Number of Households				
	Gov	District	Total Population	Proportional Allocation	Kish Rule	Kish Rule, Setting Max to 400 and Redistributing Remainder over Rest of Districts	Number of Clusters, Rounded to 0	Number of Households
1	Erbil	Hawler center	852,329	1,215	797	400	40	400
2	Sulaymaniya	Sulaymaniya center	761,557	1,086	715	400	40	400
3	Duhok	Duhok center	323,400	461	328	351	35	350
4	Duhok	Zakho	237,236	338	258	281	28	280
5	Erbil	Deshti Hawler	203,072	290	232	255	25	250
6	Sulaymaniya	Raniya	198,518	283	229	252	25	250
7	Erbil	Makhmur	178,319	254	214	237	24	240
8	Sulaymaniya	Kalar	170,624	243	209	232	23	230
9	Duhok	Semel	162,058	231	203	226	23	230
10	Erbil	Soran	159,969	228	201	224	22	220
11	Duhok	Akre	152,124	217	196	219	22	220
12	Sulaymaniya	Chamchamal	146,358	209	192	215	21	210
13	Duhok	Shekhan	145,043	207	192	214	21	210
14	Erbil	Shaqlawa	131,660	188	183	206	21	210
15	Duhok	Bardarash	118,841	169	176	198	20	200
16	Sulaymaniya	Pishdar	114,731	164	173	196	20	200
17	Duhok	Amedi	95,797	137	163	186	19	190
18	Erbil	Koye	95,746	137	163	186	19	190
19	Erbil	Khabat	95,148	136	163	186	19	190
20	Sulaymaniya	Halabja	91,611	131	161	184	18	180
21	Sulaymaniya	Sayid Sadiq	73,010	104	153	176	18	180

Table A.2—Continued

	(1)	(2)	(3)	(4)	(5)	(6)	(7)	(8)
				Number of Households				
	Gov	District	Total Population	Proportional Allocation	Kish Rule	Kish Rule, Setting Max to 400 and Redistributing Remainder over Rest of Districts	Number of Clusters, Rounded to 0	Number of Households
22	Sulaymaniya	Dukan	62,881	90	149	172	17	170
23	Sulaymaniya	Sharezur	58,536	83	147	170	17	170
24	Erbil	Mergasur	52,865	75	146	169	17	170
25	Sulaymaniya	Kifri	47,250	67	144	167	17	170
26	Sulaymaniya	Derbendikhan	43,297	62	143	166	17	170
27	Sulaymaniya	Penjwin	40,475	58	142	165	16	160
28	Erbil	Choman	28,404	40	140	163	16	160
29	Erbil	Rawenduz	22,608	32	139	162	16	160
30	Sulaymaniya	Sharbajer	18,628	27	138	161	16	160
31	Sulaymaniya	Khanaqin	11,967	17	138	161	16	160
32	Sulaymaniya	Qaradakh	7,983	11	137	160	16	160
33	Sulaymaniya	Mawat	7,839	11	137	160	16	160
Totals			4,909,884	7,000	7,000	7,000	700	7,000

NOTES:
Column (4) shows allocation across districts under proportionate allocation for n=7,000.
Column (5) shows allocation across districts under Kish rule for n=7,000.
Column (6) shows the allocation modifying Kish rule to set maximum district sample to 400 households, distributing "excess" households equally over districts under 400 households to maintain total sample of 7,000.
Column (7) indicates the resulting number of clusters/PSUs per district, rounding to allow 10 households per cluster.
Column (8) indicates the resulting number of households per district (= number of clusters x 10 households per cluster).

Table A.3
National and Subgroup Margins of Error for Labor Force Participation Rate

	Total ESS	N	Est LFP (%)	SE	Z (95)	Margin of Error (%)	95 CI Lower Bound (%)	95 CI Upper Bound (%)
Overall	15+	8,394	42.3	0.0054	1.96	1.1	41.3	43.4
Ages	15–29	4,532.8	37.7	0.0072	1.96	1.4	36.3	39.1
	30–49	2,770.0	55.2	0.0094	1.96	1.9	53.4	57.1
	50–64	1,091.2	45.4	0.0151	1.96	3.0	42.4	48.3
Gender	Female	4,331.3	14.7	0.0054	1.96	1.1	13.7	15.8
	Male	4,146.6	72.1	0.0070	1.96	1.4	70.7	73.5
Urban-rural	Urban	6,639.7	42.3	0.0061	1.96	1.2	41.1	43.4
	Rural	1,754.3	45.7	0.0119	1.96	2.3	43.4	48.0
Males	15–29	2,230.9	63.1	0.0102	1.96	2.0	61.1	65.1
	30–49	1,355.9	94.9	0.0060	1.96	1.2	93.7	96.1
	50–64	559.8	80.2	0.0168	1.96	3.3	76.9	83.5
Females	15–29	2,364.9	13.0	0.0069	1.96	1.4	11.7	14.4
	30–49	1,394.7	19.6	0.0106	1.96	2.1	17.5	21.6
	50–64	545.4	14.2	0.0149	1.96	2.9	11.3	17.1
Urban	15–29	4,342.3	36.1	0.0073	1.96	1.4	34.6	37.5
	30–49	1,806.0	52.8	0.0117	1.96	2.3	50.5	55.1
	50–64	491.3	43.4	0.0224	1.96	4.4	39.1	47.8
Rural	15–29	689.5	39.2	0.0186	1.96	3.6	35.6	42.9
	30–49	694.7	57.5	0.0188	1.96	3.7	53.8	61.1
	50–64	370.2	47.3	0.0259	1.96	5.1	42.2	52.3
Urban	Male	3,280.0	74.0	0.0077	1.96	1.5	72.5	75.5
	Female	3,426.1	12.0	0.0056	1.96	1.1	10.9	13.1
Rural	Male	866.6	76.1	0.0145	1.96	2.8	73.3	78.9
	Female	905.2	16.6	0.0124	1.96	2.4	14.2	19.0
Duhok	Male	875.5	71.3	0.0153	1.96	3.0	68.3	74.3
	Female	893.3	11.3	0.0106	1.96	2.1	9.2	13.4
Erbil	Male	1,447.3	70.9	0.0119	1.96	2.3	68.6	73.3
	Female	1,574.5	12.7	0.0084	1.96	1.6	11.0	14.3
Sulaymaniya	Male	1,728.1	79.6	0.0097	1.96	1.9	77.7	81.5
	Female	1,864.5	19.1	0.0091	1.96	1.8	17.3	20.9
Duhok	Urban	1,289.9	39.4	0.0136	1.96	2.7	36.7	42.1
	Rural	489.7	42.9	0.0224	1.96	4.4	38.5	47.3
Erbil	Urban	2,466.4	38.8	0.0098	1.96	1.9	36.9	40.7
	Rural	555.5	42.2	0.0210	1.96	4.1	38.1	46.4
Sulaymaniya	Urban	2,905.2	46.1	0.0092	1.96	1.8	44.3	47.9
	Rural	687.5	50.1	0.0191	1.96	3.7	46.4	53.9

Table A.4
National and Subgroup Margins of Error for Unemployment Rate

		N	Est UE (%)	SE	Z (95)	Margin of Error (%)	95% CI Lower Bound (%)	95% CI Upper Bound (%)
Overall		3,552	11.9	0.0054	1.96	1.1	10.8	13.0
Ages	15–29	1,707	15.3	0.0087	1.96	1.7	13.5	17.0
	30–49	1,530	8.0	0.0070	1.96	1.4	6.7	9.4
	50–64	495	9.4	0.0131	1.96	2.6	6.8	11.9
Gender	Female	638	16.5	0.0147	1.96	2.9	13.6	19.3
	Male	2,989	10.9	0.0057	1.96	1.1	9.8	12.0
Urban-Rural	Urban	2,806	12.0	0.0061	1.96	1.2	10.8	13.2
	Rural	802	11.0	0.0111	1.96	2.2	8.8	13.2
Males	15–29	1,408	14.0	0.0093	1.96	1.8	12.2	15.8
	30–49	1,287	7.6	0.0074	1.96	1.5	6.2	9.1
	50–64	449	8.6	0.0133	1.96	2.6	6.0	11.2
Females	15–29	308	21.1	0.0233	1.96	4.6	16.5	25.6
	30–49	273	9.9	0.0181	1.96	3.5	6.3	13.4
	50–64	77	13.2	0.0384	1.96	7.5	5.6	20.7
Urban	15–29	1,566	15.7	0.0092	1.96	1.8	13.9	17.5
	30–49	954	8.3	0.0089	1.96	1.7	6.5	10.0
	50–64	213	9.6	0.0202	1.96	4.0	5.7	13.6
Rural	15–29	271	14.4	0.0213	1.96	4.2	10.2	18.6
	30–49	399	7.6	0.0132	1.96	2.6	5.0	10.2
	50–64	175	8.8	0.0215	1.96	4.2	4.6	13.0
Duhok	Male	438.7	8.5	0.0133	1.96	2.6	5.9	11.1
	Female	447.6	7.6	0.0125	1.96	2.5	5.1	10.1
Erbil	Male	631.2	5.7	0.0092	1.96	1.8	3.9	7.5
	Female	686.7	7.5	0.0101	1.96	2.0	5.5	9.5
Sulaymaniya	Male	645.9	4.8	0.0084	1.96	1.6	3.2	6.4
	Female	696.9	6.9	0.0096	1.96	1.9	5.0	8.8
Duhouk	Urban	646.3	17.7	0.0150	1.96	2.9	14.8	20.6
	Rural	245.3	16.2	0.0235	1.96	4.6	11.6	20.8
Erbil	Urban	1,075.6	11.4	0.0097	1.96	1.9	9.5	13.3
	Rural	242.2	10.5	0.0197	1.96	3.9	6.6	14.3
Sulaymaniya	Urban	1,085.8	10.0	0.0091	1.96	1.8	8.2	11.8
	Rural	256.9	9.1	0.0180	1.96	3.5	5.6	12.7

APPENDIX B

Rotation Scheme for the KRLFS

Why Rotation Designs?

When carrying out repeated surveys to understand changes over time in such measures as the unemployment rate, it is advantageous to reinterview the same households or individuals. More generally, it is best to have as much overlap of the sample as possible from one period to the next. Overlap reduces the variance of the estimates of changes—it allows more precise estimates—because the individuals in the sample are the same or similar from one period to the next. In contrast, if we took completely separate samples of individuals each period, there would be a lot less correlation of outcomes across periods. The estimates of change consequently would have a higher variance.

Since changes over short periods in such outcomes as the unemployment rate may be relatively small, it is important to get the most precise estimates possible to be able to identify statistical significant changes. For example, a drop in the unemployment rate from 10 to 7 percent would be a notable improvement from a policy point of view. However, this change of 3 percent is not very large in absolute (percentage point) terms and thus requires relatively low variance to be able to establish statistical significance; the ME in the estimate of the change must be less than 3 percent to be able to say that the rates are indeed different.

These considerations might suggest that the optimal approach to repeated surveys is to return to the same households each round and to do so indefinitely (a complete overlap of the samples). However, this would lead to a significant attrition of the sample. Some of the respondents will get tired of the survey and refuse to participate in further rounds; obviously, this attrition will increase over time. One can replace those who leave with new households, but the process of dropping out may be systematic (for example, well-off people may have less patience and tend to drop our sooner). So it becomes difficult to ensure the representativeness of the sample, even with replacements. Further, households age over time, and our initial sample becomes demographically unrepresentative if it is retained for a period of years.

Rotation designs are a compromise between complete sample overlap (same households or individuals every round) and completely independent samples (households interviewed only once). They ensure statistical efficiency while avoiding serious problems with attrition. The essential aspect of rotation designs is that households or individuals are sampled for several rounds, then leave the sample permanently (they are "rotated out" of the sample). Therefore, there is significant but not complete overlap of the sample over time.

A common type of rotation design is one in which households are in the sample for a few rounds, are taken out for a few rounds, then brought back in for a few more, and finally leave the sample for good. The approach we recommended for this survey was the "2-(2)-2" rotation scheme. Each household is sampled for two consecutive quarters, then "rests" for the next two quarters, and is then sampled again for two quarters, after which they finally exit the sample. The advantage of this approach is that households are given a break for a few periods from the burden of interviewing, which helps reduce attrition. Further, the fact that households return after a gap—two quarters in this case—means that the overall period for which we observe a given cohort is fairly long (six quarters, or a year and a half)—longer than if we observed them for the four quarters consecutively (one year).

Key Aspects of the Design

Figure B.1 illustrates the 2-(2)-2 rotation scheme by showing the sampling over the first three years. There are four cohorts or panels, each making up one-fourth (1,750) of the total sample of 7,000 households. Each cohort is interviewed for two consecutive quarters, is out for two more, then back in for two more. Overlap across cohorts is achieved by staggering the addition of each cohort. Eventually, by year 2, quarter 2, four cohorts are being interviewed at once. The sample at this point thus reaches its "steady state" with the full 7,000 households and continues this way thereafter. The following are the key aspects of this design:

- Once the steady state is reached, four cohorts are sampled in each period: one completely new, one introduced in the previous quarter, one reinterviewed after having been sampled in the previous year, and one reinterviewed after having been sampled both in the previous quarter and in the previous year. For example, in year 2, quarter 3, interviewers add 1,750 households for cohort 7 (completely new); reinterview the 1,750 households of cohort 6 (interviewed for the first time in the previous quarter); reinterview cohort 3 (last interviewed in the previous year and returning after two quarters off); and reinterview cohort 2 (interviewed in the previous quarter and the previous year).

Figure B.1
2-(2)-2 Rotation Scheme for the Survey for Total Sample (n = 7,000)

Survey Round							1	2	3	4	5	6	7
		Year 1				Year 2				Year 3			
Rotation Group	Cohort/ Panel	1	2	3	4	1	2	3	4	1	2	3	4
1	1 (n=1,750)												
2	2 (n=1,750)												
1	3 (n=1,750)												
2	4 (n=1,750)												
1	5 (n=1,750)												
2	6 (n=1,750)												
1	7 (n=1,750)												
2	8 (n=1,750)												
1	9 (n=1,750)												
2	10 (n=1,750)												
1	11 (n=1,750)												

...

NOTE: Colors represent individual cohorts.

RAND *RR293-B.1*

- This means that, in each quarter, one-half of the households are kept over from the previous quarter (cohorts 2 and 6 in the example), while one-half leave permanently or temporarily and are replaced (cohort 1 leaves temporarily for its two-quarter break, and cohort 5 leaves permanently and is replaced by cohort 3, which reenters, and cohort 7, which is new). Hence, there is 50-percent overlap in the sample from quarter to quarter. This overlap helps reduce the variance in the estimates of changes over time.
- Further, the design produces a 50-percent overlap of the sample between *years,* ensuring greater efficiency in the estimation of year-to-year changes.

Rotation Groups

To manage this sampling approach logistically, it is useful to divide the sample clusters (blocks in our case) into different RGs. We proposed a system with two RGs such that, for our total sample of 700 clusters and 7,000 households,

- each RG would contain one-half (350) of the sample clusters and one-half (3,500) of the sample households.
- two of the four cohorts sampled in a given quarter would belong to RG 1 and two would belong to RG 2.

A two-RG strategy like this is used, for example, in the Palestine labor force survey.

We started creating the RGs as follows. Our note on sampling discussed stratification by district, and a two-stage design (choose clusters or PSUs, then households within them). According to our modified Kish approach, different numbers of clusters were to be randomly selected within the districts for the first stage. To create the two RGs, we operated as if we wanted to create two samples, each one-half the size of the final sample of 7,000 households in 700 clusters. Therefore, we selected clusters from the districts according to the allocation given in the sampling note but did so twice, each time selecting one-half the number of specified clusters from each district.

For example, if a district was assigned 22 clusters, we randomly selected 11 blocks from the district and assigned them to RG 1. Then, from the remaining blocks in the district, we randomly selected another 11 and assigned these to RG 2. Thus, we ended up with two RGs with 350 blocks each, with each district having its clusters divided evenly between RG 1 and RG 2.

To see how this works, refer to Figure B.1. In the first quarter, we choose cohort 1 by sampling 1,750 households from RG 1. Given that RG 1 is a set of 350 blocks, we select five households randomly from the household listings in each cluster in RG 1 (to yield $350 \times 5 =$ 1,750 households).

In the second quarter, cohort 2 is added from the RG 2 clusters. In each of these clusters five households are randomly selected. Cohort 1 is also interviewed a second time.

In the third quarter, cohort 1 leaves on its two-quarter break, while cohort 2 is interviewed a second time. Cohort 3 is newly added to the sample from RG 1; five new households are added from each of the clusters in RG 1 to form the 1,750 households of cohort 3. Note that *households in the new cohort are added from the same clusters from which the older cohort*

(cohort 1) is being removed. This is because they are both in the RG 1. This pattern occurs regularly in this scheme and has statistical implications discussed later. In practical terms, in each of the RG 1 clusters, we need to randomly select the five new households from the listing of households *excluding* those chosen for cohort 1, since cohort 1 households have already been interviewed for two rounds and are now on a two-quarter break. The cohorts must be mutually exclusive groups of households.

In the fourth quarter, cohort 4 is added from RG 2. At the same time, cohort 2 leaves RG 2 for its two-quarter break. Again, cohorts leave and enter the sample from the same clusters. Therefore, the five households for cohort 4 are randomly selected from the household listings for these clusters *excluding* the five households that are already in cohort 2. Cohort 3 is interviewed a second time.

The process continues as in Figure B.1 until year 2, quarter 2, when we would have built up to the full sample of four cohorts and 7,000 households. After this point (the steady state), to elaborate on the properties discussed in the section "Key Aspects of the Design,"

- Four cohorts are interviewed in each quarter.
- Two cohorts are from RG 1, and two from RG 2.
- In each quarter, one-half of the sample, or two cohorts, from the previous quarter is reinterviewed. These two cohorts are from the same RG.
- In each quarter, one-half the sample, or two cohorts, leaves and is replaced by two cohorts from the same RG.

Two points should be made. First, the fact that a cohort of households that exit the survey is replaced by a new cohort of households in the same clusters is significant. While this may help with management and recordkeeping, the main purpose is statistical efficiency. As noted above, overlap over time in the sample improves precision because of correlation across periods. The strongest correlation occurs, of course, when the same households are in the sample across periods; this is known as primary correlation. Since we have a rotating panel, this complete overlap is not possible. However, some efficiency gains can be obtained if households that enter are from the same clusters as those that leave. This occurs because of correlations among households within the same cluster, which are expected to be similar in various ways (as discussed with the ICC and the DEFF in our sampling note). Therefore, there is a benefit from a weaker correlation, known as a secondary correlation, if new households are selected from the same location as households that are leaving the sample. This explains our particular setup of the RGs.

A second point has to do with the fact that the new cohorts are being drawn from the same groups of clusters over time. As indicated above, the new cohort should be randomly sampled from the list of households excluding those that have already been in the survey, to reduce respondent fatigue. If we are determined not to use households beyond the single cycle for one cohort, the pool of available households for new cohorts in the cluster gets smaller and smaller over time. Therefore, at some point, a new sample of clusters would need to be drawn from the sampling frame; that is, the first stage sampling will have to be repeated.

Starting the Survey with a Complete Sample

The process described above was an incremental building up of the sample quarter by quarter as one new cohort is added each quarter, resulting in a full sample of 7,000 households and four cohorts only by the sixth quarter of the survey (year 2, quarter 2, in Figure B.1). While this process is relatively straightforward to implement, it has the disadvantage of not yielding the ultimate sample size for some time, so estimates up to that point (e.g., of the national unemployment rate) will be less precise than desired.

However, it is possible to begin with the full sample by starting off *as if* the survey was in year 2, quarter 2 (shown as survey round 1 in Figure B.1). We recommend this approach so that the survey can produce reliable estimates in the first round itself. This is done as follows:

1. Create the two RGs as discussed above.
2. From each cluster of RG 1, randomly select five households for cohort 1. Then, from the list of remaining households in these clusters, randomly select five households to be in cohort 5.
3. From each cluster of RG 2, randomly select five households for cohort 2. Then, from the list of remaining households in these clusters, select five households to be in cohort 6.
4. All the above households (n = 7,000) are interviewed.

In the next quarter, we act as though we are in year 2, quarter 3 (see Figure B.1) and treat each cohort accordingly:

- Cohort 1 is treated as though it has already been interviewed four times by the previous quarter, so leaves the survey.
- Cohort 2 is treated as though this quarter is its fourth interview, so continues for this round and then leaves permanently.
- Cohort 5 is treated as though the previous quarter was its second interview, so it leaves this quarter to return two quarters later, for two more survey rounds.
- Cohort 6 is treated as though this is its second interview, so after this quarter, it takes a two-quarter break before returning for two more survey rounds.
- Cohort 3 is started in RG 1 clusters (five new households per cluster). We will treat this cohort as though it is coming back after being interviewed twice and then out for two quarters, so it will be interviewed again next quarter and then leave permanently.
- Cohort 7 is also started in RG 1 clusters (five new households per cluster) for the first of its four survey rounds.

We continue this approach for the next several quarters.

References

Angel-Urdinola, Diego F., and Kimie Tanabe, "Micro-Determinants of Informal Employment in the Middle East and North Africa Region," Washington, D.C.: World Bank, January 2012. As of November 23, 2013:
http://documents.worldbank.org/curated/en/2012/01/15763718/
micro-determinants-informal-employment-middle-east-north-africa-region

Berry, Sandra H., Nicholas Burger, Harun Dogo, Krishna B. Kumar, Alessandro Malchiodi, Jeffrey Martini, Tewodaj Mengistu, Howard J. Shatz, Alexandria C. Smith, Artur Usanov, and Joanne K. Yoong, *Designing a System for Policy-Relevant Data Collection for the Kurdistan Region–Iraq*, Santa Monica, Calif.: RAND Corporation, MG-1184-KRG, 2012.

Central Agency for Public Mobilization and Statistics (Egypt) CAPMAS, website, 2013. As of November 25, 2013:
http://www.capmas.gov.eg

Central Bureau of Statistics of Syria, website, undated.

Eurostat, *Task Force on the Quality of the Labour Force Survey: Final Report*, Luxemburg: Publications Office of the European Union, 2009. As of November 25, 2013:
http://epp.eurostat.ec.europa.eu/cache/ITY_OFFPUB/KS-RA-09-020/EN/KS-RA-09-020-EN.PDF

International Monetary Fund, "Dissemination Standards Bulletin Board," website, 2012. As of November 25, 2013:
http://dsbb.imf.org

Iraq Household Socio-Economic Survey–IHSES-2007, website, January 2009. As of January 31, 2014:
http://web.worldbank.org/WBSITE/EXTERNAL/COUNTRIES/MENAEXT/IRAQEXTN/0,,contentMD K:22032522~menuPK:313111~pagePK:2865066~piPK:2865079~theSitePK:313105,00.html

Kingdom of Bahrain Central Informatics Organization, "The Bahrain Industrial Production Survey for Manufacturing Establishments," website, 2007. As of November 26, 2013:
http://www.cio.gov.bh/cio_eng/SubDetailed.aspx?subcatid=255

Kish, Leslie, "Multipurpose Sample Designs," *Survey Methodology*, Vol. 14, No. 1, 1988, pp. 19–32.

Statistics New Zealand, "New Zealand Annual Enterprise Survey 2010/2011," website, 2011. As of November 26, 2012:
http://www2.stats.govt.nz/domino/external/quest/sddquest.nsf/12df43879eb9b25e4c256809001ee0fe/e54943 cd044ac240cc2579210075be08?OpenDocument

Turkish Statistical Institute, website, undated. As of November 25, 2013:
http://www.turkstat.gov.tr/

The World Bank, *Iraq Household Socio-Economic Survey*, 2007. As of December 3, 2013:
http://web.worldbank.org/WBSITE/EXTERNAL/COUNTRIES/MENAEXT/IRAQEXTN/0,,contentMD K:22032522~menuPK:313111~pagePK:2865066~piPK:2865079~theSitePK:313105,00.html